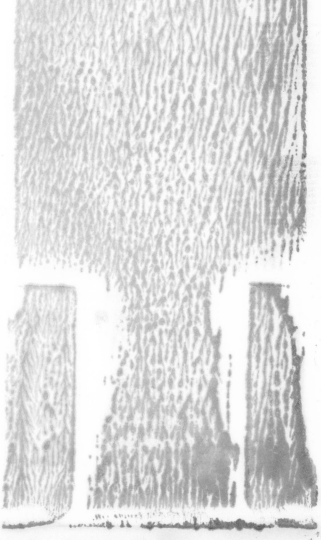

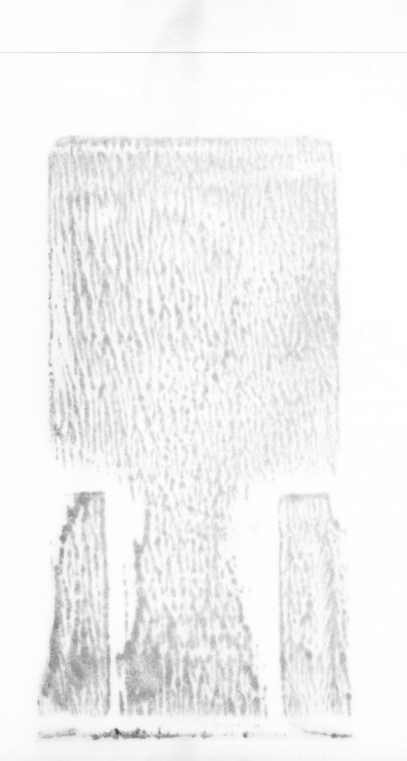

TEACHING
THE RETARDED READER

TEACHING
THE
RETARDED READER

A Guide for

Teachers, Reading Specialists, and Supervisors

STELLA M. COHN

Director, Special Reading Services
Board of Education, City of New York

JACK COHN

Supervisor
Board of Education, City of New York

THE ODYSSEY PRESS, INC., NEW YORK

To our son, Cal

PREFACE

Many inquiries have come to the authors from classroom teachers, reading specialists, teachers preparing to become reading specialists, and supervisors regarding the teaching of the retarded reader. These numerous inquiries prompted the writing of this book. This book has been planned as a resource for the reading specialist, the remedial reading teacher, the reading consultant, and the staff of a reading clinic. For the classroom teacher, this text should serve to help her in her efforts to teach the retarded reader. For teachers working with adults for whom English is a second language, this book may also have many values.

The materials presented are the result of many years of experience by the authors in their work with disabled readers. There has been no attempt to cite works of others or summaries of research completed elsewhere but rather to present a practical approach. The authors present the thinking of recent research in the field and have added to this their own reflections.

This book describes the details of the work of each of the different disciplines involved in improving the reading of the retarded reader. There are numerous forms and job analyses which have been developed and represent many years of practical experience. During this time there were adaptations and modifications resulting in the present forms and job descriptions. These are intended to serve as elaboration, occasionally as clarification, of the material in the text. They may be found to be of value in other situations than those described. These forms and job analyses and illustrations are integral parts of the text.

We wish to express a special acknowledgment to Margaretta Fite, a psychologist assigned as supervisor, who shared so generously of her creative thinking and her experience. To the many staff members with whom the authors worked over the past decade we extend our deep appreciation. They offered suggestions and shared their knowledge of effective procedures for teaching the disabled reader—all of which helped us to formulate and crystallize our thoughts.

It is hoped that this book will serve as a guide for those involved in upgrading the reading level of the retarded reader.

S. M. C.

J. C.

CONTENTS

ILLUSTRATIONS

TEACHING
THE RETARDED READER

1 WHO IS THE RETARDED READER?

The retarded readers are students for whom learning to read presents marked difficulty in spite of their being equipped by chronological age and general intelligence to benefit normally from instruction. They are members of all kinds of families. Some of their parents are illiterate; some speak only a very little English; but others are widely read and some are college graduates.

Retarded readers appear in all kinds of schools—private and parochial as well as public. Contrary to opinions rather generally expressed, pupils with reading difficulty are not new to this generation nor to this century. However, as the tendency to classify children in more or less homogeneous age groups has become widespread, more of the pupils who have failed to learn to read are in the upper elementary grades and in the secondary schools than formerly. This is because they are usually held back only once in the primary grades, where they used to be retained year after year as unhappy misfits, often dropping out of school at an early age. Now, with the enforcement of compulsory education laws, they cannot escape school entirely. An appreciable number of truants, however, still come from the ranks of poor readers; and it is to prevent this type of mal-adjustment that reading specialists and clinics work persistently with the "hard core" cases, and find success with the great majority.

It is the authors' experience that at least twice as many boys as girls are referred for help. The fact that a higher percentage of boys than girls has severe difficulty with learning to read has been known for a long time, though the reasons for this are still not definitely established. One explanation is that at the age of school entrance and during the period when reading instruction is first begun, most boys are physically less mature than girls in ways which affect response to instruction. Boys seem less able to conform to the routine of the schoolroom and to being controlled by the teacher. The greater restlessness of the six-year-old boy and his apparently greater need to assert physical prowess and to get satisfaction from vigorous outdoor play may militate against his giving optimum attention to the paper-and-pencil activities which are ordinarily used to develop "readiness" for reading.

Another opinion is that reading difficulty in many cases is based on obscure organic defects which adversely influence perceptual-motor behavior required for reading. These defects may be more prevalent among boys than girls, like other deviations, for example, left-handedness, defective color vision and speech defects.

Perhaps psychological as well as physiological factors favor the girls so that more of them are able to accept reading instruction and to respond well from the beginning. As girls, they more naturally look to the woman teacher as model and want not only to please her but to be like her. Is reading difficulty on the part of the pupil with normal potentialities for learning essentially a behavior disorder, and more common to boys than girls, as is other problem behavior, especially in the category of rebellion against authority? Is the expectation of society—of parents as well as the school and the larger community—that girls when first entered in school will conform, will do what is wanted by adults and so will learn—is this a generally motivating force for girls? And conversely, are anxieties and doubts regarding the little boy's educational future more frequent ingredients of his environment and thus productive of a generally negative influence on his first responses to reading instruction? Further research is required for answers to these and other pertinent speculations.

One of the authors participated in an analysis of the findings of thirty-five cases which had been diagnosed and evaluated by a psychologist, a social worker, a psychiatrist, and a reading clinic teacher. Available for this investigation were the confidential case records which contained the social history, the psychological findings (including the results of projective testing, as well as measurements of the intellectual functioning), and the report of the psychiatric examination. Prior to this analysis, each child's response in the reading room had been fully reported by the reading teacher in a series of anecdotal reports. In addition there were school records, the class teacher's observations, and the results of examinations by the pediatrician, the ophthalmologist, and the speech improvement teacher.

Based on this analysis a profile of a typical reading disability child was developed. This child would be male, nine years old, and in the fourth grade. He would have at least average intelligence—usually above average intelligence—and probably would be doing nearly as poorly in arithmetic as in reading. In the classroom he would appear to suffer from severe anxiety, hyperactivity, depressive trends, and fearfulness. He would usually have periods of excessive daydreaming and distractibility. These symptoms occurred in two-thirds of the cases. In his early school history the pupil would probably have had no kindergarten experience and various unfortunate school experiences, such as frequent changes of school or teachers, serious illnesses, and excessive absences.

In the typical pupil in the study, occasionally other problems such as speech defects and variations of visual acuity might be further handicapping factors. These physical and developmental factors then, while they do not appear crucial in the origin of the reading problem, are contributory.

Whether they are boys or girls, however, the children with reading disabilities are generally characterized by failure to respond well to beginning instruction in the first grade. Their individual histories show that they have had an undue number of unhappy experiences in the period preceding and during attendance in the first grade. Most of these disturbing events did not originate at school, though they often led to interruptions of school attendance (as from prolonged or frequent illnesses and from accidents) and to changes of school. Many other experiences were traumatic in an emotional sense, having to do with changes in the home situation or with disturbed relationships severe enough to result in "school phobias" or other evidences of maladjustment at school.

With very few exceptions, the parents of the pupils with reading problems do express an interest in their children's schooling and want them to do well. Many have taken an active role in trying to help them to learn to read; they are not consciously neglectful, no matter what their own educational experiences have been. However, very few express confidence or hope regarding these particular children. On the whole they are disappointed and discouraged. They compare them unfavorably with siblings. Frequently they consider them dull or even mentally retarded. These feelings are inevitably conveyed to the children. Parental anxiety—as much as annoyance or outright anger—often spells lack of love to a child. As a result, the child feels unwanted and fails to develop a normal feeling of self-worth. His reactions will differ from others' in accordance with individual differences which have developed during his pre-school experiences; with other attributes of his physical, intellectual, and emotional make-up; and with the values he has begun to assimilate from his family and other associates. Many children, fearing their parents' withdrawal of love, are motivated by the unconscious need to remain infantile or to regress to infancy; thereby in effect assuring continued close parental care. Examples are: failure to outgrow infantilisms in their speech, a return to bed wetting, the development of food fads, failure to cooperate in following prescriptions for wearing glasses, etc. If the parents continue to give excessive personal supervision to the child's daily routine behavior, they tend to discourage his normal growth toward independence. Overprotection of a child usually provides only a facade of love, making the ineffective child cling more grimly to his symptoms of maladjustment (including reading failure). If the parent punishes angrily, the child may only become confused further as to the nature of his fault. Sometimes the infantile behavior, having been so well learned, is retained by the child and psychosomatic problems are added—such as overweight, underweight, and the exaggeration or prolongation of minor ailments. Such difficulties can and do occur in homes ordinarily described as normal.

It is important to determine the degree and depth of service that is needed for each of these retarded readers. Such an analysis will help in planning the program as regards the pupil and parent. For some students a carefully worked out program of remedial instruction is adequate; for others some interview and counseling sessions for the parent should be an integral part of the program. For the more intense cases it will be necessary to provide not only remedial reading but also a clinical service where the social worker will counsel and/or treat the parent and the psychologist will examine and, where necessary, treat the child.

The social worker may have to spend a good deal of time with the parents, in helping them to realize that the child's symptomatic behavior has a relationship to their feelings and attitudes. Only when this is accomplished is it likely that their own more serious problems of family life are revealed and the social worker can either provide the necessary treatment or find outside sources of help. Such treatment can ultimately change the climate in the home and free the child from the unfavorable pressures coming from parental conflict and anxiety so that he can develop in healthy ways toward his own fulfillment—both educationally and socially.

Knowing the details of the problem is not enough. Equally important is the understanding of the specific ways in which both child and the members of his family who are closest to him attempt to effect adjustments. Having insight into the specific mechanisms which the pupil is using to try to satisfy his basic needs helps the therapist or reading teacher to use appropriate methods in dealing with him. What has caused the poverty of ideas, the meagerness of information, the ignorance of ordinary concepts of time and space (especially knowledge of the local community) which characterize pupils with reading difficulty? These lacks also represent in the pupil of normal intelligence an unwillingness to reach out beyond the self with the independent effort which is required for learning.

The boy or girl with reading disability—and related problems—is the boy or girl who is still engrossed almost exclusively with himself. He has not learned how to relate to his peers nor to the adult world, usually because the problems of parent-child relationship have not been solved. If as a result he is afraid, he may withdraw; if angered he may fight— with his fists or with words; if very seriously deprived or frustrated, he may also resort to fantasy and live in an unreal world. Whether in economically deprived or affluent circumstances, such are the students with reading difficulty. Normal in intelligence (some above average in potential) they reveal many different symptoms in addition to the reading failure.

Not to be overlooked, however, are the positive elements which seem never to be completely lacking in a child's situation—no matter how deprived his life has been. It is most important to find out, from the pupil's record of experience, at school and at home, evidences of positive interests or aptitudes which can be utilized constructively by both the reading teacher and parents to motivate behavior which will build up the child's self-image. Often the educationally defeated pupil, once he is stimulated to make the effort to create or achieve something in line with a positive interest of his own, encouraged by the reading teacher and accepted by the parents, looks at himself with new confidence and at this point begins to learn.

2 CONSIDERATIONS FOR
AN EFFECTIVE PROGRAM
OF REMEDIAL READING

It is important to clarify our viewpoint concerning reading difficulty. Reading disability cannot be looked upon simply as a failure that can be laid at the door of the school. Poor teaching is not generally the basic cause of reading disability, though at times it is an important contributory reason. As a matter of fact, there are relatively few cases of pupils whose reading difficulty can be traced directly only to an inadequate method of instruction. There has been found no single pattern of causative factors underlying reading failure. Nor is there any evidence in the enormous literature on this subject to indicate a unitary cause. Continued difficulty in learning to read on the part of a student of normal intelligence is the outcome of many adverse factors within the child, his home, and his school environment. The student brings all of himself to the reading act—his strengths and his liabilities. It is important to assess them. It is this assessment which should determine the nature of the program to be developed for the individual pupil.

An overview of remedial reading programs in different school systems and clinics reveals that almost every known approach is used. The different remedial reading programs vary from the purely phonic approach to the use of machines exclusively. Each protagonist for a particular program persists in saying that his success is due solely to the method used. This can be confusing to teachers seeking to learn the most effective procedures.

It is true that many of these programs do succeed with a considerable number of pupils. This points up the fact that there must be some commonality in these distinctly different programs whch brings about these favorable changes in the disabled reader. Experience in working with the retarded reader has shown that the reading problem is the result of a constellation of factors. It is also significant that cases of reading disability are seldom identical and consequently must be viewed as requiring different instructional programs. The causative factors contributing to the reading disability are also seldom the same in any two cases.

What then is the difference between a remedial program of reading and the classroom teaching of reading? Many of today's teachers have been trained in the fundamental principles of teaching, of child development, of an understanding of the needs of pupils and of mental hygiene procedures, of the factors concerned with reinforcement of skills, of the basic importance of motivation, and of the significance of pupils' interest. Good classroom teaching has many aspects of the procedures found effective in a remedial reading program. Certain basic considerations should serve as guidelines in providing an instructional program for students with reading disabilities.

2.1   DIAGNOSIS

A sound program of remedial instruction requires a careful diagnosis in order to determine the strengths and needs of each pupil. Students with reading disabilities frequently have uneven patterns of development. Some pupils may have learned the skills of recognizing unfamiliar words but have little skill in comprehension; others may have no background of experiences with which to develop a meaningful vocabulary.

In a careful diagnosis, the reading teacher not only learns what skills and knowledges the pupil has not learned but also what learnings he has acquired incorrectly. With this information, the reading teacher plans the instructional program to help the students master the materials they failed to learn originally and to reteach those knowledges and skills learned incorrectly. As the program continues, the reading teacher needs to test the pupil again to analyze what has been mastered, what needs to be re-emphasized, and what new learnings should be planned. This diagnosis of the pupil's reading should serve to guide the teacher in determining what procedures are most effective in helping pupils master the needed skills. In effect, the continuing diagnosis serves two purposes. The most important function is to analyze the pupil's learnings in order to continue to plan appropriately for his instructional needs. A further outcome of this ongoing diagnosis by the reading teacher is to help her evaluate the effectiveness of her instructional practices.

It becomes apparent as the program of remediation moves forward, that as needs are met, and the pupils master the materials, other difficulties arise and new needs have to be dealt with. The plans for instruction change or become modified based on these changing needs. What has been described as suitable for a program of remedial instruction certainly applies to effective classroom procedures. (For further details on diagnosis, see Chapter 3, p. 12.)

2.2   THE READING TEACHER— THE REMEDIAL READING TEACHER AND THE READING CLINIC TEACHER

The question is frequently asked: "What kind of teacher are you looking for?" The most direct fundamental reply to this question is: "A teacher who feels good inside about children." This teacher must be sincere, warm, and fond of children with all their foibles. Without these basic ingredients, the other considerations become insignificant. Experience in teaching in an elementary or secondary school for not less than three years is an essential requirement for the reading teacher; specialized preparation through graduate courses in the teaching of reading should also be required.

A reading teacher must guide students into believing that she believes they can learn to read. She must convey to them her belief in their ability and intelligence to master this reading act. She knows that these are students who view themselves as failures; they have failed their parents, their teachers, and themselves. They need to be helped to develop new and different feelings about themselves and their capacities. A sensitive, exciting teacher can create situations which will enable the pupil to see

himself in a more accepting light; will create situations in which the
pupil can experience a new sense of self-worth and self-respect.

2.3   MATERIALS OF INSTRUCTION

The reading teacher must select materials that "fit" the reading level of
the student and that are of interest to him. As the reading teacher is
getting to know her pupils, she is learning about their special interests.
With this knowledge, the reading teacher selects materials centered
around the interests of the boys and girls.

In selecting the level of difficulty of the material to be used, it is
suggested that the material be at a somewhat lower level than the pupil's
general reading achievement. This is important for two reasons. First,
standardized tests usually give a maximum score of the pupil's achievement. Second, it insures that the boys and girls will experience some
success in attempting to master the skills.

Along with commercial materials, teacher-prepared materials are often
very helpful and useful. Such materials can be developed around the
specific skill needs and interests of the pupils. The reading teacher may
find these materials more effective in motivating these pupils to want to
read. (A more detailed account of "Materials of Instruction" appears in
the chapter, "The Reading Clinic Program" on p. 54.)

2.4   MOTIVATING THE RETARDED READER

The boy or girl with a reading disability can only associate unhappy
feelings with reading and wants to avoid these unsuccessful experiences.
He appears to dislike reading and books. He views himself as "not much
good" and even fears that he may be quite stupid. He feels that he is not
like other pupils. He is sure that something is different about him.

The reading teacher's most important task in her earliest relationships
with these boys and girls is to remotivate them. She must help them to
know that she believes they can learn to read and then so guide them

that they too will also begin to believe that they can learn to read. The disabled reader must gain new faith and confidence in himself. He needs to feel that he is accepted. Successful experiences may help him to change his feelings about himself and about reading.

The reading teacher through her relationships and attitudes will convey her appreciation, her faith, and her confidence in him. In helping him to begin to recognize his reading problem, to analyze it, and to plan with the reading teacher ways to overcome it, the pupil will begin to gain new confidence in his ultimate success in mastering reading. Periodic pupil self-evaluation is an important factor in remotivating the retarded reader.

2.5   THE INSTRUCTIONAL PROCEDURES

The essential differences between regular classroom instruction and remedial instruction is in the depth quality of the diagnosis and in the highly individualized instruction rather than in the method used. Teaching procedures which have been found to be sound in the classroom also apply to the remedial reading program.

The remedial program is not narrow in any sense that suggests that any one method or approach is to be used. Since disabled readers are not identical and since it is generally agreed that a reading disability is not the result of a unitary causative factor, the method or approach selected must be the one most effective for that pupil. For some, a phonic approach may be suitable; for others an individualized reading program and for still others a kinesthetic method may be best. In general for most boys and girls with reading problems, a program of enrichment and experiential learnings should be included.

The reading teacher should plan regular periodic conferences twice a month with each pupil's classroom teacher, and, on the secondary level, with the English or other assigned teacher. This will set up lines of communication so that there will be continuous exchange between the classroom teacher and the reading teacher. During these conferences, the diagnostic findings, the procedures that have been found to be most effective, and some of the materials used are described and shared with the classroom teacher. In turn, the class teacher discusses the pupil as regards the classroom situation. These conferences should provide an opportunity for an exchange and sharing of knowledge about these boys and girls and their learning experiences and other significant information and should result in cooperative planning to meet changing needs.

2.6 THE FAMILY

In analyzing data of many of the pupils with reading problems, it is not uncommon to find that some of the home situations contributed to the reading difficulty and, in some instances, were the source of the disability. Therefore, shortly after a child is accepted into a remedial program, it is advisable for the reading teacher to meet with the parent.

During this initial conference the nature of the program is described to the parent and the reason for the pupil's need for this special help program is explained. Then as the conference continues it is important to ask the parent what she thinks may have brought about the reading difficulty. Such information, if obtained, may be helpful in understanding the pupil and may serve to point the way for future conferences. It is important to involve the parent and to help her see her role in this program.

The parent should be guided into becoming more accepting of her child or less protective or demanding, depending upon the situation. In most cases it is inadvisable to have parents assume the role of tutor or supervisor of the pupil's work. It has been found that in some instances where the parents cannot accept the idea that their role as tutor is ill-advised, it may be better for such parents to give them some very specific simple learnings to work on with their child.

In general, parents should be encouraged to read to the boys and girls; to make attractive books available; to provide varied and different experiences such as excursions, trips, and visits to libraries and museums. A sound program for remedial reading should include the parent as an involved and active participant in helping the pupil to improve his reading.

3 DIAGNOSING THE RETARDED READER

In discussing the diagnosis of a learning disability, the question is frequently raised regarding the intensity or depth of the diagnosis. This is dependent on many factors. Primarily, the very nature of the reading disability is the basic consideration; secondly, how much of the teacher's time can be made available for this; thirdly, how much training has the teacher had; fourthly, what other resources are available to assist in this diagnosis.

When a physician diagnoses a patient, he generally has two goals. He wants to find the possible causes which have contributed to or produced the present symptoms and then to determine the appropriate treatment for this. A reading diagnosis should determine the reasons for the pupil's reading difficulties through careful analysis and then prescribe procedures for improving or overcoming the difficulty. The multiplicity of causes underlying the reading problem of retarded readers frequently react upon one another, thereby compounding the problem.

3.1 DIAGNOSIS SHOULD INCLUDE ALL ASPECTS OF THE PUPIL AND THE READING ACT

3.1.1 PHYSICAL FACTORS

Physical factors, although sometimes insignificant in nature, may affect the pupil and his learning ability. Any discomfort will reduce the student's effectiveness in the classroom situation. Some major physical factors to be considered are defective vision, speech and hearing, glandular imbalance, and neurological problems.

There are many kinds of visual defects which contribute to difficulties in reading. The major ones are nearsightedness, far-sightedness, astigmatism, and muscular imbalance. In some learning situations a hearing defect is more a contributory factor to the reading disability than in others. Where it is known that a pupil has a hearing defect it is important for the teacher to emphasize a visual approach to reading.

In regard to the area of speech defects, again the sensitive teacher will focus on a visual approach rather than stress oral reading and phonics. In addition, a program of speech therapy should be provided.

Pupils suffering from glandular disturbances are frequently obese and lethargic or hyperkinetic and very much underweight. Such defects require appropriate medical attention. Neurological examination should be requested for pupils who have deformity of the head, poor equilibrium, general awkwardness, extreme restlessness, and a history of seizures.

There is another group of boys and girls who manifest problems in dominance or have directional confusion. Either of these difficulties frequently may interfere with learning to read. In examining the research studies concerned with lateral dominance and success in reading it is apparent that there is conflicting data. Several studies report that there is no constant relationship as regards handedness, eyedness, reversals, and reading achievement.

In one of the author's work with boys and girls in reading clinics, most of the pupils with problems of dominance or directional confusion were able to overcome these difficulties and achieve success in reading through good instructional procedures.

3.1.2   INTELLECTUAL FACTORS

The use of the group intelligence test is under close scrutiny in some quarters. There are some who believe that it is not a sound educational practice to compare intelligence and reading achievement. They believe that many group intelligence tests are measures of specific reading abilities. Group intelligence tests do penalize poor readers and consequently do not estimate their mental ability accurately. In New York City, the use of the group intelligence test in the public schools was recently suspended.

In selecting pupils for a remedial reading program, it is important to include primarily those pupils who are average or above average in intelligence. The authors believe that a program of remediation in reading should not substitute for a modification of curriculum for those students whose reading difficulty is one aspect of a slower developmental process. In Chapter 4, on page 24, appears "A Guide to Teachers' Estimates of Intelligence of Pupils Retarded in Reading." This should help teachers evaluate pupil's intelligence.

3.1.3   PERSONALITY FACTORS

Teachers have sometimes noted that two pupils in a class may demonstrate similar problems of personality, yet one is a successful reader while the other has many reading difficulties. This is true and sometimes complicates the diagnostic process.

In an analysis of cases in the reading clinics of New York City Public Schools the findings were grouped under the following categories: (1) symptoms of disturbance in the pupils; (2) problems within the family; (3) situational factors in regard to early school experiences; and (4) adverse physical and developmental findings. The data showed that many of these factors were common to a majority of the pupils. However, no two cases were identical, and in no instance was the reading retardation the only problem.

The incidence of symptoms of disturbance within this group of pupils was as follows:

100% showed excessive anxiety
80% had excessive fears

69% were children who spent much time daydreaming
66% had depressive tendencies
46% showed severe disruptive behavior
46% showed infantile behavior

Reading failure in itself is a very serious problem but these boys and girls were also carrying a load of many other unsolved problems. One thing is certain—if a remedial reading program is to be effective, the reading teacher must know these pupils as individuals and must understand them. A diagnosis must include an assessment of the pupil, his relationship with his classmates, with members of his family, and with his teachers. It is important to know how the pupil feels about himself and how he sees his reading problem. It is the competent, sensitive teacher who learns to look behind the student's behavior and to observe and gather information and insights about his responses. If a more intensive diagnosis is necessary, then a clinical work-up may be indicated.

3.1.4 ENVIRONMENTAL FACTORS

It has been estimated that more than 50 percent of the children with reading disabilities come from maladjusted homes. Such factors have their bearing on the pupil and his attitudes. This is information which will help the teacher understand the pupil's attitude.

Parents can serve to stimulate children's interest and enrich their experiences—all of which frequently serves to help children learn to read easily and happily, providing there are no other interfering forces. It is also important to know what the parental attitudes are towards the child's reading disability. If these attitudes are overprotective, anxious and pressuring, critical and negative as regards his learning abilities, they will contribute towards his continuing failure.

The reading teacher must get to know this student, become familiar with his feelings about himself, and evaluate his environmental influences. She should observe the pupil in the playground, during testing, in group relationships, and also when he is alone. She should observe him to determine how he sees himself and his reading failure, how he responds to success, and what special interests he has. Then, having gathered these facts, the reading teacher will analyze them in relation to the reading act. The reading teacher will attempt to provide rich and varied experiences in reading and an opportunity for the pupil to taste success.

3.1.5 EDUCATIONAL FACTORS

Poor teaching, an unhealthy emotional climate in the classroom, unsuitable materials of instruction, inadequately prepared teachers are causative factors that may contribute to reading difficulty. In some cities, a very serious problem confronting the school personnel is the high incidence of pupil mobility. Similarly, the staff shortages and the frequent turnover of staff, a problem of recent years, is contributing towards pupils' learning difficulties, especially in reading.

The reading teacher studies the pupil's educational history (through examination and analysis of the pupil's records) and she notes his attitudes towards school. While these factors may not be of major significance in themselves, they are clues to the student's total school experience. The diagnostician (reading teacher) gathers the data and adds them to her own direct observations and other analyses.

3.2 DIAGNOSIS SHOULD BE CONTINUOUS

In medicine, a diagnosis is made to determine the causes for certain symptoms and then a prescriptive program is set up either to remedy or to eliminate the symptoms. Such diagnosis may be continuous. Similarly, in education, a diagnosis is made and plans for a program of remediation prescribed. In education, diagnosis must be continuous. In part this is so because new learnings often depend on the already learned skills and knowledges. This then places a responsibility on the educator and especially on the reading teacher. She must ever be alerted to new and changing growth of these boys and girls.

There should be periodic evaluations of the pupil's reading development. For those pupils who are making progress, it is necessary to provide further diagnosis so that new needs can be recognized and planned for For those students who do not appear to be undergoing any perceptible changes, it may be necessary to use additional measurements or supplementary appraisals and evaluation techniques.

3.3 DIAGNOSIS SHOULD INCLUDE PLANS TO IMPROVE THE READING ACT

No study of a retarded reader can be complete, although much comprehensive information and data have been collected, without a plan to provide a program of remedial or corrective procedures. If there are problems in the immediate environment that are contributing to the reading disability, plans need to be set up to improve, overcome, or help the student adjust to them. Similarly, the reading teacher will set up a plan to help the pupil experience success; help him gain approval; guide him to better relationships with his peers; help him to become involved in his reading problem, if these appear to be his needs. There should be a continuous follow-up of the pupil's physical problems to insure that corrective procedures are working.

3.4 DIAGNOSIS SHOULD INCLUDE INFORMAL PROCEDURES AS WELL AS STANDARDIZED TESTS

In making a diagnosis, in addition to environmental, behavioral, or physical problems contributing to the reading difficulty, it is essential to analyze the reading disability and proceed to correct it. This may be done by informal as well as formal procedures. In using the informal approaches, the reading teacher should proceed as systematically as possible. This informal procedure is often most helpful when the diagnostician (reading teacher) wishes to make a further study of some specifics that were observed in the formal procedure. The sensitive reading teacher is ever seeking an understanding of the ways in which the student attempts to effect adjustments—the specific mechanisms which he is using to try to satisfy his basic needs. This knowledge of the student helps the reading teacher in the selection of appropriate methods and procedures in dealing with him.

A careful analysis of the pupil's reading disability not only helps determine the nature of the reading disability, but should also point up the specific weaknesses in skills. This analysis should also include the instructional plans for overcoming these weaknesses. (See section, "Reading Diagnosis," in Chapter 4, "The Reading Clinic Program.")

3.5 DIAGNOSIS SHOULD BE LIMITED TO THE SPECIFIC NEEDS OF THE INDIVIDUAL PUPIL

If diagnosis is to be properly determined, the first steps must be to ascertain the causes of the reading difficulty. When this is done, the depth of this diagnostic procedure will be related to the underlying causes. For some pupils, a measurement of general reading ability and some measure of mental ability will be adequate. Where there seems to be evidence of physical problems, it will be important to provide the pupils with an intensive physical examination. For some of these pupils, the examining physician or staff members may request a neurological examination. Where the student is showing behavioral problems in conjunction with reading difficulties or where a study of causes of the reading disability cannot be readily determined, a psychological examination may be indicated. The difficulties of some of these students may be so complicated as to require an intensive study by the psychologist, parental conferences with the social worker, conferences of the clinical staff with the reading teacher and the classroom teacher, and a diagnostic evaluation by the psychiatrist.

The forementioned procedures describe the kinds of individual diagnoses that should be provided. Fundamental to all of this is the fact that the study of the pupil's reading problem must be related to demonstrable pupil needs.

4 THE READING CLINIC PROGRAM

4.1 AN OVERVIEW OF THE PROGRAM

4.1.1 GOALS AND OBJECTIVES FOR A READING CLINIC

These objectives are concerned primarily with help to the disabled readers referred for service and secondarily with communication of general findings which are thought to be important. The first three objectives motivate all of the work with pupil, parent, and teacher. The fourth objective, which concerns the outcomes, serves to analyze their meanings in order to increase understanding of reading disability and to indicate how it can be dealt with in a school setting.

For the pupil: To improve his attitude toward reading, to raise his level of achievement in reading, and to bring about a more favorable personal-social development.

For the parent: To help parents develop insight into the emotional and reading problems of their children and to obtain their active cooperation in the effort to help their children.

For the classroom teacher: To help the teacher to recognize the nature of the problems of the individual pupil with reading disability and to explore ways in which she can contribute in this effort to help the pupil.

For the school, the community: To communicate through reports, conferences and seminars pertinent insights or techniques obtained.

4.1.2   ESTABLISHMENT OF A READING CLINIC

The establishment of a reading clinic entails the selection of a school or other building that has adequate space to house the staff. It should be so located that it is easily accessible for parents and children. The reading clinic becomes a permanent facility. Much consideration needs to be given to the location in terms of transportation. Whether parents and children are going to use public or private transportation, it is essential that careful planning include an exploration of the routes, the public means of conveyance, etc.

4.1.3   STAFF

If possible, a reading clinic program should have the following positions:

1 Director
3 teachers of reading
1 school psychologist
1 school social worker
½ day per week of the services of a psychiatrist
1 stenographer

(For reading clinics having a supervising psychologist and a supervising social worker, a description of these positions appears in the section, "The Clinical Program.")

The instructional staff members should be selected on the basis of demonstrated competence in reading instruction and aptitude for dealing with the emotionally disturbed student.

4.1.4   A TYPICAL READING CLINIC

The reading clinic center usually should contain at least three reading rooms; offices are for the Director, the stenographer (with space for records, supplies and telephone), for the social worker, who also needs a telephone; and for examining and treatment rooms for use of the psychologist and psychiatrist.

If possible, space for the reading clinic should be built into a school setting. The advantages are many. Working with emotionally disturbed boys and girls in a reading clinic has been found to be more effective when the clinic is housed in a school setting. The pupil is less resistive. Parents are more readily motivated to come and to keep appointments.

SUGGESTED PLAN FOR A READING CLINIC

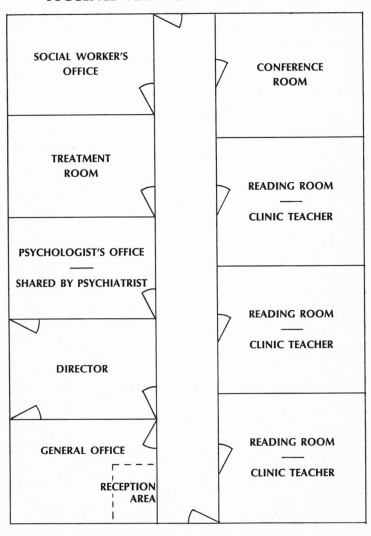

SOCIAL WORKER'S OFFICE

CONFERENCE ROOM

TREATMENT ROOM

READING ROOM
—
CLINIC TEACHER

PSYCHOLOGIST'S OFFICE
—
SHARED BY PSYCHIATRIST

READING ROOM
—
CLINIC TEACHER

DIRECTOR

READING ROOM
—
CLINIC TEACHER

GENERAL OFFICE

RECEPTION AREA

4.1.5   COOPERATIVE SELECTION OF THE PUPILS

Boys and girls are referred by the principal and, in smaller communities, service may be requested by the parent. The number of referrals should have some relationship to the number of vacancies. In general, the number of pupils the principal refers to the reading clinic should not be more than can be accepted. Usually, in reading clinics serving elementary children, schools tend to refer pupils when they are in the fourth grade, or third grade, probably because reading failure at this level makes it almost impossible for the boy or girl to participate in an increasingly complex curriculum. It is also recommended that second graders with reading difficulty be referred.

Within this framework the following criteria for selection apply:

1. Reading retardation of at least one and one half years if the boy or girl is in fourth grade, and correspondingly greater or less retardation if the pupil is in a higher or lower grade than fourth.

This evaluation of reading retardation is approximate, rather than strict in a numerical sense. Grade scores resulting from standardized silent reading tests involve a certain amount of error. Other factors to be considered are the nature of the pupil's difficulties in both oral and silent reading, as observed by the reading teacher, and in the judgment of the class teacher. Though in the main the pupil's reading achievement is compared with expected competence for his grade placement, his chronological age, school history, and estimated mental maturity must also be taken into account in assessing his need for clinical help.

2. The pupil's need for help in personal-social adjustment.

Generally, these are students who have shown behavior disorders or evidences of incipient personality difficulties which are related to their reading failure. Boys and girls who are retarded in reading simply because of long illness or other situations resulting in loss or delay in schooling, usually are able to make up for such gaps in instruction by utilizing the resources available in the classroom. The clinical and instructional staff of a reading clinic is needed for helping students for whom poor reading is one symptom of underlying difficulty.

3. Parental willingness to cooperate actively with the social worker. This includes parental consent for medical and ophthalmological or optometric examination, and also for psychiatric evaluation, if indicated.

The parent is expected to keep scheduled appointments with the social worker, at which time problems relating to the family and child—directly and indirectly—are explored; and, if possible, worked out. In the intake interview the parent agrees in writing to have a full diagnostic study including examination of the child by the psychiatrist, if needed.

4. Evidence that the pupil has at least "average" mental ability.

The reading clinic program is designed to meet the needs of the child whose reading achievement is markedly below that which is characteristic of others of his mental maturity. It would be desirable to have an individual psychological examination, including an intelligence test, of every pupil referred. However, when caseloads are heavy and intake large, psychological services need to be limited. To avoid extending the time taken for the selection process, other means must be found for estimating the pupil's potential ability. The purpose is to exclude only the truly mentally retarded and "borderline" pupil whose reading difficulty represents not a special problem but merely one aspect of a slower developmental process. The instructional program of the reading clinic is not planned as a substitute for the necessary curricular modifications needed by the boy or girl of low intelligence. On the other hand, it is most important to locate the many pupils with true reading disability who have been mistakenly regarded as mentally retarded. Psychologists, whenever available, will examine doubtful cases. Usually, class teachers' estimates of a pupil's potential for learning are taken into account. These class teachers may be assisted in their observations and evaluations of pupils referred to the clinic by reference to an outline prepared for this purpose. On the following page appears "A Guide to Teachers' Estimates of Intelligence of Pupils Retarded in Reading."

The integrated work of the instructional-clinical team is well illustrated by the procedure followed in the selection process. After the pupil has been referred, the reading teacher takes the first steps in accumulating needed information on each pupil. She studies the school records, interviews the class teacher and other school personnel, talks with the student, gives him appropriate reading tests, and summarizes all of this

A GUIDE TO TEACHERS' ESTIMATES OF
INTELLIGENCE OF PUPILS RETARDED IN READING

The class teacher can provide information from her observations of the intellectual functioning of the pupil. As a guide to the teacher's effort to evaluate the intelligence of the retarded reader, it will be helpful to note whether the pupil

........has evidenced good learning capacity in certain activities not dependent upon reading—special interests, hobbies, school subjects like mathematics, construction work.

........shows better vocabulary development in conversation than in reading.

........observes and points out essential aspects of things; e.g., in the case of pictures, objects, social situations, ideas.

........notes similarities and differences; is able to utilize comparisons and contrasts in thinking.

........detects absurdities in situations; e.g., in cartoons, stories or happenings in real life.

........comprehends meanings, sees implications or offers interpretations of experiences.

........demonstrates ability to plan activities and foresees probable happenings.

........remembers facts which are important or significant.

........solves problems by logical or systematic methods.

If a pupil with reading disability has shown that he can function normally in several of the above, he appears to have the potential to acquire the skills of reading appropriate to his age level. On the other hand, if he appears to function normally in very few of the above, and resources permit, an individual examination by a psychologist should be arranged.

information on a special selection data form. If the pupil does appear to meet the criteria from the instructional point of view, the case will be forwarded to the social worker and psychologist, who will proceed with the initial clinical study. A more detailed account of the selection process appears in a later section.

On the facing page appears the "Selection Data" form.

SELECTION DATA

Date_____   Reading Teacher_____

School_____Class_____Teacher_____ Room_____

Names: Pupil_____Father_____

Language spoken at home _____.Mother_____
Maiden Name   First Name

Address_____Telephone_____.

Birth date_____Birthplace_____Number of siblings_____

First school entrance: School_____Year_____Grade_____

Attendance: Days of absence for each year

Kg_____1_____2_____3_____4_____5_____6_____7_____8_____9_____10_____

No. of transfers_____.

Sensory defects: Visual problem (Underline)   Yes   No   Corrected
Glasses: lost or broken

Hearing difficulty (Underline)   not apparent   suspected   verified

Health_____

Teacher's evaluation: Personality_____

(Record additional data on back of page)

Outstanding trait or problem (opinion of present teacher)

Parents' attitude toward school_____

Tests: Intelligence tests: Date and I.Q. for each

Group tests:_____ _____Individual tests: S.B._____ _____

WISC_____ _____Other tests:_____ _____

Examined by:_____

Math: (Percentile)_____ Date_____

Reading Scores:

Reading Readiness (percentile)_____ Date _____

Other tests: Name of test_____ Form_____

Scores_____ _____.Date_____

Scores_____ _____Date_____

Examiner_____

Disposition of Case:

4.1.6. ORIENTATION OF NEW STAFF

In the selection of staff there are several guidelines. They should have had experience in the classroom where they have been better than average teachers. They also should have demonstrated an interest in the teaching of reading and be willing to further this interest by continuing to take courses, participate in conferences, and keep abreast of the most recent literature in the field. They should also have shown special skill in working with the troubled pupil.

As for the clinical personnel, here too the experience of working in an agency concerned with boys and girls and families is very important. With this background, the clinician is better able to deal with the pupils and their learning problems. Nevertheless, for all new personnel, regardless of their years of experience, an orientation program should be set up at the beginning of the school year. Of course, if it is necessary to bring in new staff during the year, the Director must plan a program to familiarize the new staff members with the reading clinic and his or her role in it. As an integral part of the orientation program, the last sessions should be devoted to observation of the program and discussions. Below is listed an outline of an orientation program that has been used with new staff:

Outline of Sessions of an Orientation Program

Session 1
  Introduction
    Team approach—reading clinic teachers, psychologists, social worker, and psychiatrist

Session 2
  Selection procedures
    Criteria for the selection of pupils
    Screening by the reading teacher and clinic team

Session 3
  Diagnostic procedures
    Identification and interpretation of reading needs, physical, social, and emotional needs
    Diagnostic tests
    Informal reading inventory
    An Analysis of Reading Difficulties (form)—its use and interpretation
    Evaluation of diagnosis

Session 4
Grouping for instruction: factors to be considered
Grouping should be flexible

Session 5
The role of the social worker
The role of the psychologist
The role of the psychiatrist

Session 6
Planning for instruction
Motivation
Aims: specific skills
Procedures
Outcomes

Session 7
The instructional program
Readiness
Word recognition skills
Selling a book

Session 8
The instructional program (continued)
Dictionary skills
Comprehension skills
Use of table of contents, index
Use of reference material

Session 9
Research skills
Widening of students' reading interests, refinement in reading tastes, and greater use of books and libraries

Session 10
Role of the classroom teacher, English teacher, or special teacher (the latter two in the higher schools) in this team approach

Session 11
Record keeping
Pupil folder—(see section on record keeping by the reading clinic teacher)
The writing of anecdotal records

Session 12
Evaluation procedures

All sessions should provide an opportunity for questions and discussion. This program as outlined should take a week to complete. It is advisable to have another day devoted to discussion of problems and unanswered questions after the staff member has been at work for about three months.

4.1.7 INSTRUCTIONAL ASPECTS

Planning for an out-of-classroom program of reading instruction for disabled readers depends upon the answers to certain questions: *why? who? where? when?* and *how?*

The first two questions of *why* the program was established and *who* the retarded readers are, have been considered in the preceding pages, which have dealt with the policy for the reading clinic program. The remaining questions relate specifically to the organization and functioning of the instructional program.

The question of *where* the boys and girls would be instructed is determined to some extent by the size of the community. In smaller communities pupils should be serviced at the reading center to which they come or are brought. In larger communities many different factors require consideration. The pros and cons of transferring elementary pupils into this center, if it is housed in a school, for their entire instructional program needs careful consideration. Such a plan provides for the concentration of resources—both clinical and instructional—in the center school. It is also felt that the service could be spread more widely in this way. This possible arrangement has serious limitations. Boys and girls are traveling out of their neighborhoods to reach the center school. This cannot always be arranged. These boys and girls need to be accompanied to a distant school. Many parents are unable to provide transportation because of financial reasons and others are not available to accompany the student because of being employed or needing to care for younger siblings. Also, a large reading clinic center, in which boys and girls from many schools are given service, simply removes problems from the referring schools, and fails to give assistance to local school personnel in understanding and working with disabled readers due to lack of communication. This lack occurs because the reading clinic staff is functioning apart from the schools where pupils are in attendance.

The second alternative of having the students brought to the center school only for periods of reading instruction on two days per week also entails problems regarding transportation, and has the additional disadvantage of separating them from their classrooms for approximately twice the length of the reading period. Moreover, many of these maladjusted boys and girls might become overstimulated or otherwise disturbed by these trips. In addition, one very important aspect of such a service, namely, continuing communication with the classroom teachers, cannot be maintained in such a plan.

The following is a plan used most effectively in a large school system. However, some smaller school system may find this more feasible, too. The plan which appears to be most satisfactory in practice is one in which the reading teacher services two schools and forty or more children each week. Thus a fully equipped reading room which can also be used for consultation with and demonstration for class teachers is available in each of the cooperating schools. The advantages of such a plan are many— including the more efficient use of the pupils' time and the absence of the other disadvantages listed above. The reading teacher, in effect, becomes an auxiliary member of the staff in the two schools. She can arrange for more flexible grouping in accordance with the development of the students, and can change her schedule at times to adapt to special assembly programs, other scheduled periods, or events in the individual school which none of them should miss. Under this plan, classroom teachers are also more readily available for conferences about individual students.

The question of *when* the pupils should be seen for reading instruction —that is, how many times a week—has to be decided on the basis of opinion, since, so far as is known, there has been little research on this subject. Precedent favors meeting young pupils daily for group instruction. Several years ago, a study was conducted by one of the authors to ascertain the effectiveness of four reading sessions and two reading sessions per week. This study is reported on below.

A Study—Optimum Number of Reading Sessions per Week

At one of the reading centers, the author experimented with a four-period week for one year, followed the next year by a doubled caseload on a two-period week. When reading scores were compared, it was found that the pupils receiving two periods per week gained as much as those given four periods. This was conducted with one and the same reading teacher thus eliminating the variable of having different teachers. The reading teacher attributed this unexpected result to observations that the pupils whose time was shortened seemed to place a higher value on the special reading sessions, showing more anticipation of a lesson and eagerness to get to work. It was also felt that the boys and girls needed more time between sessions to absorb the skills and knowledges acquired in these intensive small group sessions. Three sessions per week appear to provide optimal conditions for remedial reading instruction. However, for the most efficient deployment of staff, two periods weekly has proven satisfactory.

4.1.8 CLINICAL ASPECTS

The disabled reader needs to be studied and his learning difficulties evaluated not only from an instructional but also from a clinical point of view. The clinic team needs to gain insight into the pupil's total life situation, including the inner life of his feelings and his needs. As mentioned earlier, a clinic should have provision for a social worker and a psychologist to share the responsibility of the clinical caseload. They work together to coordinate their diagnostic and treatment services for parents and children. In those cases which require intensive diagnostic study and planning for treatment, the clinic team may use the services of a psychiatrist for consultation and diagnosis. The psychiatrist may also provide treatment for selected pupils—either by individual or group therapy.

An important aspect of the clinician's work is consultation with the Director, the reading teachers, and other school personnel.

4.1.9 THE AUXILIARY SERVICES

The reading clinic program should seek to take into account the broader life situation of the children and their parents, recognizing that the factors contributing to reading disability are varied and may be multiple. For example, an important part of the intake study should include a medical examination for each child. This could be arranged with the school doctor or family physician. The clinic social worker should obtain from the parent a detailed social, medical, and developmental history of the child. Where necessary and in accordance with the medical report, referral for ophthalmological, and/or optometric or neurological study is made by the social worker or the school nurse. In cases where special treatment is recommended, the social worker should help the parent to follow through.

On the following pages appears the form, "Medical History and Physical Examination Record."

Because many pupils with reading difficulty have a history of delayed or defective speech, it is important to have a speech diagnosis for each one and, if there is a Speech Improvement Teacher available, her cooper-

MEDICAL HISTORY AND PHYSICAL EXAMINATION RECORD
(Special Referral Examination)

Name_____Date of birth_____Class_____ School_____

Parent or Guardian _____History taken by_____Date_____
(Social Worker or
School Nurse)

Family History (significant facts)

Father_____Mother_____

Siblings: age and sex_____ _____

_____ _____

Pertinent family illnesses or diseases _____

_____

Past History

Prenatal_____Delivery_____

Birth weight_____Condition at birth_____

Early feeding_____

Development_____

Illnesses, operations, accidents_____

Present Health

Habits: Eating_____Sleeping_____

Nail biting_____Bed-wetting_____

Unusual activities_____

Handedness_____

Eyedness_____

ATTENTION SCHOOL PHYSICIAN: Please add to the above history as indicated.

PHYSICAL EXAMINATION (List positive findings)

Parent present— Yes ( ) No ( ) Soc. Worker present— Yes ( ) No ( )

Weight_____lbs. Height_____in.

Estimate of nutritional status_____Skin _____

Posture (if poor, describe)_____ Spine and extremities_____

Head_____Ears and hearing _____

Eyes (state in all cases)   L   R

    Vision—Before correction   ( )   ( ) Date of screening_____

           After correction   ( )   ( ) Date of eye exam._____

Other_____Referred for ophthalmological and/or optometric exam.
                        Yes ( )   No ( )

Nose and sinuses_____Mouth and pharynx_____

Neck_____Lymph nodes_____

Chest_____ Lungs_____

Heart_____

Abdomen._____Genitalia (male only)_____

General behavior_____ Evidence of emotional instability_____

Gait_____Muscular coordination_____

Deep reflexes_____Superficial reflexes_____

Additional_____

Heel-knee, finger-nose_____Abnormal movements_____

Remarks and Summary

Recommendations:

Date_____   Signature_____
                                            (Physician)

ation should be obtained in providing these examinations. Every pupil in a reading clinic should have a written report from the Speech Improvement Teacher, to be kept in his instructional folder. In cases where the speech difficulty requires direct attention by the specialist, speech therapy should be carried on. The many opportunities for oral expression in the small reading group may incidentally lead to an improvement of the pupil's speech. Also, where both the reading and the speech difficulty are symptoms of the same underlying problems, a clinical approach to the parent and the child may be the effective method.

4.1.10 CLINIC DAY AND THE TEAM APPROACH

Unique to the reading clinic program is the close working relationship of the instructional and clinical staff members. In the initial phases of screening, admission, and orientation of the child and the parent to the service, there should be a sharing of functions by the reading teacher and the clinic team. The reading teacher should have considerable information regarding each pupil's reading problem, his school history, and the impression of him as given by his former and present classroom teachers. The clinicians, from their studies of parent and child, should be able to throw some light on the dynamics underlying the pupil's reading failure and other problems. Some of these contributing factors may be physical, neurological, cultural, and psychological. Information will almost always be available on the pupil's assets—for example, his interests and special abilities. In the initial review of findings regarding a particular student, the social worker should contribute information regarding the parent's view of the reading problem, of the pressures within the family, and the possible strengths which could be utilized in dealing with parent and child. The insights gained from this type of conference should enable the team of clinicians and reading teacher to work out the best approach to meeting the pupil's learning and personality needs.

A particular day of the week should be designated as "clinic day." One of the most important aspects of a reading clinic program should be the ongoing teamwork of clinicians and instructional staff. The sharing of thinking and experiences of these disciplines makes such a program unique.

On this day personnel of the instructional and clinical staffs should meet at the clinic center. Conferences should be planned in advance, each reading clinic teacher having submitted the previous week the names of those students she wishes to discuss. The social worker or psychologist may also request a conference on a particular boy or girl. A summary of the referral question or problem, the discussion, and the recommendations made are recorded following each conference.

One important value in this close integration of work is that staff members of different disciplines support each other by different approaches to the same problem, and by the common acceptance of goals.

4.1.11   "GRADUATION" AND THE "ALUMNI ASSOCIATION"

As students reach grade level or better in reading, and have shown sufficient growth in personal-social adjustment to be able to maintain themselves without further assistance from the reading clinic, the staff should begin to prepare them for leaving the program. A "graduation" exercise might be held in which the "graduates" participate in a simple program. Parents of the children might take part in this. In order to provide a means for follow-up, the "graduates" should become members of the "Alumni Association" and meet twice a month with the reading teacher. The members of the "alumni" should be tested at the conclusion of each year to determine whether they are maintaining themselves adequately.

4.1.12   ARTICULATION WITH THE NEXT HIGHER SCHOOL

In the spring, conferences should be held between the staff members of the reading clinic and guidance counselor of the next higher school to transmit essential data concerning the pupils. These conferences should also serve to plan the most effective class placement for each boy or girl needing special consideration. In some schools it may be possible for the staff members of the reading clinic to participate in the completion of the articulation cards.

4.1.13   RECORD KEEPING

Many facts about the pupil and his situation are accumulating concerning the period before as well as during the time he spends in the reading clinic. It is not sufficient to gather facts. They must be organized and recorded in such a way that they may be used efficiently. Records should contain accurate, significant data which can be of continuous and cumulative value to the administrative, clinical, and instructional staffs. Adequate instruction, counseling, and treatment can be given only when pertinent data is readily available.

For each individual student in the program there should be a confidential clinical folder, described later in this chapter in the section, "Record Keeping by the Clinical Staff."

There should also be another pupil folder maintained by the reading clinic teacher which includes an anecdotal record, reading test results (and test booklets), a speech diagnosis, and numerous other data which have to do with the pupil's reading diagnosis and progress, described later in this chapter in the section, "Record Keeping by the Instructional Staff."

4.1.14 COOPERATION WITH THE STAFFS OF THE SCHOOLS AND OTHER PROFESSIONAL PERSONNEL

By virtue of its original goals, planning and organization, a reading clinic should function as an integral part of the school(s) where retarded readers are serviced. There should be ongoing communication by the reading teachers and clinicians with the class teachers and supervisors, both in conferences regarding individual pupils and also in faculty meetings where more general aspects of the reading program are discussed. Each reading teacher should confer twice a month with the class teacher of every pupil on her caseload. This will provide considerable opportunity for sharing problems and for offering suggestions regarding causative factors and desirable methods of dealing with those who have reading difficulty.

A dual purpose is implicit in this type of communication—primarily, the furtherance of benefits which such cooperative work brings to the individual pupil with whom the reading clinic is concerned, and secondarily, in the teacher education aspects which should also accrue to the total school program. An example of one phase of teacher education to which the reading teachers may make many contributions is through their demonstrations. These teachers of reading should be called upon in this way to assist the newly assigned teachers, or others with special needs. Provision for observation of the reading instruction should be arranged by the school supervisor. The various types of individually prepared instructional materials and commercial materials should also be available for study and use by the classroom teachers.

The reading clinic also has a responsibility to publicize its work with retarded readers to other professional personnel outside the community. It is in this way that they will not only serve pupils and parents, but also the community at large. Such visitations should be arranged through the Director. The Director should arrange for observations in the reading room and conduct conferences before and after the observations.

4.1.15   RESEARCH

Research should be one objective of a reading clinic program. Even though no special personnel are assigned to carry out a systematic program, a research point of view should be prevalent in the thinking of the staff members. Research should be carried on by reading clinic staff members in the course of work on their Ph.D. dissertations. They should be encouraged to plan investigations of problems having theoretical and practical interest. Graduate students from local colleges should be assisted in research studies with pupils in the reading clinics. Such projects may entail cooperative work by numerous staff members, both clinical and instructional. As a result of such investigations, some of the findings should serve to enrich the staff's understanding of the work with pupils having reading disability.

4.1.16   END-TERM EVALUATION

When students are accepted by a reading clinic no time limitation should be set in advance as to the length of their stay. This is because of the many individual differences in the pupils, not only in the severity of the reading problem but also in intellectual capacity, motivation toward reading, emotional stability, health aspects, and all of the familial and other environmental factors tending to favor or inhibit learning to read. Reading growth usually proceeds at an accelerated pace when the many adverse factors enmeshed with the learning difficulty can be unravelled and more positive elements strengthened. Thus the reading teacher's aims, procedures, and achievements should not be restricted to concern with reading growth alone. Nevertheless, just as the symptom of reading failure in such pupils is the major focus of the reading clinic program, so the measurement of reading gains provides the most tangible evidence of progress; and the end-term use of standardized reading tests is established policy for purposes of evaluation.

Usually during May or early June, the reading clinic teacher should consider each pupil's reading skills as manifested in his recent work and decide upon his probable reading grade level. On the basis of this judgment a test suitable for him should be selected. A testing program is carried out by the reading clinic teacher.

The results of the achievement tests should be analyzed for two purposes; one, to evaluate the progress of each individual pupil in the program and two, to provide statistical data regarding the reading progress of the total group of students.

Each pupil's test results should be considered in the light of his response in the reading group and also by comparison with the evaluation obtained from his class teacher. The latter should be consulted by the reading teacher, who is seeking information not only regarding the pupil's reading progress but also concerning his personal-social adjustment. The interview need not be structured, but questioning may proceed somewhat as follows:

Has there been evidence of positive change in the pupil's attitude toward reading and other school subjects?

Has there been growth in the pupil's relationship with his classmates? Is he better integrated with the group? Is the group accepting him?

Is the pupil showing evidence of increased participation in classroom activities?

What problems does he present?

The reading teachers should summarize the end-term findings and record them in the anecdotal record of each pupil, where they may be considered in future instructional planning. Here the findings are also available to the clinicians working with the child and his parents. In many cases, conferences of the team of workers should be held which may then result in recommendations to the school principal regarding questions of promotion or classification of a particular student.

Apart from the use of end-term evaluations in the guidance of individual pupils, the test results and related numerical data should be summarized and analyzed statistically.

It is suggested that towards the end of the school year, usually in May, each principal whose school has been serviced by this program be asked to submit an evaluation of the total service. In this way, the Director and the staff can assess the strengths and limitations of the program and make changes and modifications accordingly.

4.2   THE INSTRUCTIONAL PROGRAM

4.2.1   AIMS AND PURPOSES

A major goal underlying the reading clinic teacher's work is to bring about a reorientation of each pupil, so that he wants to read and feels that he can read. This is an ambitious goal—in effect looking toward a transformation of the pupil from one who holds extremely negative attitudes toward school and toward himself to one who becomes interested in learning and looks upon himself as capable. The experienced reading clinic teacher can accept this goal because she has seen evidences of very favorable changes taking place in these boys and girls in both reading achievement and in personal-social growth. For newly appointed reading clinic teachers, the orientation program is designed: (1) to help them accept this goal, and (2) to guide them in the methodology which is recommended. Other reasons why the reading teacher can retain a hopeful attitude toward the eventual progress of the pupils are: (1) that they have a background of successful experience in teaching reading with emphasis on the developmental approach, and (2) that they are assured that in the clinic program they have available the help of the Director as well as of the clinicians, who share the same overall goals as they do and are concerned with the same pupils. In general, the reading teacher's confidence in the theoretical and practical effectiveness of this reading program is essential to its success.

A more specifiic objective of the reading teacher's work is to gain insight into each individual's reading problem both from a cross sectional and a longitudinal view. No matter how slight the pupil's possession of reading skills may be, it is to the reading teacher's advantage to have a clear awareness of them. Her aim with each boy or girl is to evaluate his resources on the basis of testing and also of observation during the processes of teaching. From his responses, she notes how he learns, what stimulates and interests him, what is retained, and where the greatest difficulties or resistances seem to occur.

Thinking in more longitudinal terms, the reading teacher aims to instill in all these boys and girls a love of books as well as efficient reading habits. She tries to get to know the pupil as an individual and to establish a relationship in which there is mutual confidence and liking. Once a pupil is accepted for reading help, the reading teacher's attitude toward him seeks to reflect her belief that he is capable of making progress and that she knows how to help him. Even when it may be appropriate to urge the pupil to greater effort and to say frankly that his work to date does not represent his best possibilities, this needs to be done in a context of hope, encouragement, and generally good feeling.

4.2.2. THE WORK OF THE READING CLINIC TEACHER

As stated in "An Overview of the Program" at the beginning of this chapter, there are three reading teachers in the typical reading clinic. The reading clinic teacher's major assignment concerns the selection and instruction of fifty students—that is, an official caseload of forty students and a provisional caseload of ten. This latter group of upper-grade children is given a short-term "crash" program designed to help them prepare for admission to the next higher school. She sets up and maintains a reading room in which the pupils are instructed in small groups and which also serves as a reading resource room. This is suitable for conferences with teachers and for demonstration lessons or observations, which are given in response to requests by the school principal or other supervisors. It is thus evident that the reading clinic teacher must be competent to carry out this instructional program in the special education of retarded readers and also to participate in various ways in teacher education.

In those instances where a boy or girl in the reading program is making less than expected progress, possible causative factors are reviewed and efforts are made to determine what impedes learning. The reading clinic teacher utilizes a variety of instructional approaches and periodically evaluates the relative merits of each for the individual pupil. Informal reading experiences also provide diagnostic data. Oral reading, silent reading, and written responses to teacher-prepared and commercial materials afford additional information on the pupil's reading difficulties.

In cases where a boy or girl in the reading clinic program does not make the usual initial spurt of improvement, and where little or no reading progress is made during the first few months, it may become necessary to review the case by the clinic team. This should be followed by joint planning with some deliberate efforts made to find new approaches to the pupil and/or his family. (Further information appears in the chapter, "Diagnosing the Retarded Reader," p. 12.)

4.2.3 GROUPING AND SCHEDULING

Many factors must be taken into consideration in the assignment of students to reading groups. An ideal group might be thought to be one in which the pupils are of about the same age, in the same grade and similar in the extent of their reading retardation. Even these more or less objective criteria cannot always take precedence over other matters. The schedules of the school and the program of the class teacher must be taken into consideration. Since the aim is to achieve full and eager participation, as well as maximum interest on the part of the pupil, it would be unwise to deprive him of health education, of arts and crafts, or class trips, or of any programs the omission of which would seem to the pupil or to his teacher to be a deprivation. When a reading group is made up of boys and girls from several classes, complications in the way of scheduling are, of course, multiplied. It is advisable in such cases to cooperate closely with the class teachers, in order to provide for the best interests of each pupil. Basically, the aim is to place in the same group, pupils who can be expected to work together with increasing success, both in terms of reading achievement and in social adjustment. Usually, this will mean placing together those who do not differ by more than one school grade or by one and a half years in age. Since a certain amount of trial and error is necessarily involved, the reading clinic teacher usually tells the pupils when they are first assigned that the groups are temporary, that others will probably join and some may be moved, until the best group is found for each one.

Sometimes the sex of the pupil is an important consideration in grouping the boys and girls in the middle and upper grades. Girls, who are in the minority in the usual caseload, need careful placement. It is almost never advisable to have only one girl in a group of boys, since in such a case she may remain at a distance from the rest of the group in basic interests. Also, one girl, if she is noticeably deviant and perhaps more mature physically and socially, may stimulate provocative responses on the part of the boys which limit, or at least postpone, the development of good working relationships in the group. On the other hand, the same girl might be able to participate much more happily and successfully in an all girls' group. This is not to say that such pupils' general education would be better planned in homogeneous sex groups, but only that for the very limited time of two hours a week in the reading room, it is desirable to facilitate rather than hinder the formation of groups which have a community of interests.

What is true of the group assignment of the girl with behavior or personality difficulties is also true of the more typical boys. They need to be assigned with regard to the problems as well as the positive qualities of their group members. Otherwise, they remain on the fringe of the small group, or are merely tolerated, just as they are in the classroom. It is because boys and girls with reading disability customarily have so many other problems which are entangled in their learning difficulties, that the educator who undertakes to teach them must also be "counselor"—in point of view, in background of experience, and in the creative handling of the individual and the group.

Some exceptional pupils who are too disturbed to work in a group are seen individually until such time as they are able to function in a group setting. Such individuals are fewer in number than might be anticipated, but when a real need exists for the one-to-one relationship between pupil and reading clinic teacher, in a protected setting, there is no substitute for this temporary arrangement as a preliminary to the group program.

As the reading clinic teacher works with each group, she becomes aware of the differences among these boys and girls in their rate of learning, in the development of social relationships, and in their assumption of responsibilities. Pupils who have "outgrown" their groups are then moved to groups where they will be stimulated and more highly motivated to work up to their fullest capacity. While it is manifestly more effective to make changes by "promoting" pupils to more advanced groups, sometimes misfits also develop in a group and should be placed elsewhere. It is desirable, of course, to arrange this so that positive motivation for the change will be experienced by the pupil.

4.2.4 PLANNING INSTRUCTION

Prior to the beginning of every week, the reading clinic teacher develops instructional plans for each of her groups. Except for the current and preceding week's plans, all are filed in the office of the clinic.

Goals are determined for each pupil in the group in terms of his diagnosed reading needs. Knowledge and insights regarding the pupils' personal-social development as well as their expressed areas of interest are important factors in the planning of lessons. Of course, when pupils bring in materials and raise good questions which also interest other members of a group, the creative teacher plans a lesson or a series of lessons around such a topic of mutual interest. Activity of this sort which is initiated by the boys and girls usually arises in a reading group only after it is already fairly well established. At the beginning of her work with a new group, a reading clinic teacher may have to supply all of the creative effort herself. She must be prepared to provide not only the actual reading materials but to suggest related experiences and information. She cannot count on a normal flow of questions or discussion from these pupils, for the typical retarded reader is so constricted in his mental activity, and his emotional concerns are so narrowly self-regarding, that he at first depends entirely upon the reading clinic teacher for the direction of his efforts. She therefore needs to plan her work in a good deal of detail with illustrative material which will serve to underline essential meanings and worthwhile concepts.

It is good if some part of a lesson can comprise an experience which will be remembered. In planning an experience, the reading teacher must insure that the activities involve reading, provide for skill development and culminate in the reading of books. A dramatization project, with parts to be read by the selected players, is better than one where a requirement for memorization is made. The use of puppets to illustrate expression of feelings or ideas in a story which has been read in the group may be a good plan and serve to reinforce important meanings; but the reading clinic teacher, aware of her time limitations, will be wise to use easily designed puppets, or commercially available ones, rather than take the time of the group for more elaborate constructions.

By her ability to take account of each individual pupil's needs and at the same time keep a unity of structure in the lesson for the group, the reading clinic teacher helps these disabled readers to feel a sense of identity with the group. If a wall chart or a blackboard exhibit is developed around a topic, and each pupil participates in some way in the preparation of the exhibit, it should be labeled and featured as the work of the entire group, rather than of any one individual. As a result, a formerly uncommunicative or isolated pupil may be heard to boast to a visitor examining an exhibit, "My group did that."

The reading clinic teacher's lesson plans, filed in the office, should contain rather detailed outlines of all these diverse activities. Ideas are thus available for sharing, or for their suggestive value to other reading teachers. On the facing page is a copy of the form, "Lesson Plan."

Specific aspects of the reading clinic teacher's work are described under the topics of this section and are also summarized in the "Job Analysis of the Reading Clinic Teacher," which follows.

LESSON PLAN

School_____ Name_____ Date_____

Groups	Motivation	Aims Specific Skills	Procedure

JOB ANALYSIS OF THE
READING CLINIC TEACHER

Each reading clinic teacher carries a caseload of about fifty children. These children are given two one-hour sessions of instruction weekly.

1. *Instructional Program*

    1.1 Conferring with principals regarding:
        1.1.1 Selection of pupils
        1.1.2 Progress reports
        1.1.3 Participation in faculty conferences
        1.1.4 The planning of individual and group conferences with teachers
        1.1.5 Demonstration lessons for teachers and visitors
        1.1.6 Providing instruction to groups of six to eight pupils
    1.2 Identification of pupil needs through:
        1.2.1 Standard diagnostic procedures
        1.2.2 Informal examination of pupil's reading competence
        1.2.3 Observation of pupil's functional reading
        1.2.4 Pupil interviews
        1.2.5 Conferences with clinic team regarding pupil's familial and emotional needs
    1.3 Conferences with clinic team regarding:
        1.3.1 Gaining further insights into pupil needs
        1.3.2 Understanding and evaluating pupil's changing emotional needs and adjusting the program to meet these needs
    1.4 Planning the instructional program based on:
        1.4.1 Pupil's diagnostic needs and interests
        1.4.2 Clinical findings
    1.5 Grouping for instruction based on:
        1.5.1 Pupil's achievement level
        1.5.2 Pupil's diagnostic needs
        1.5.3 Pupil's personality needs
        1.5.4 Pupil's size, sex, grade level, and fixed school schedules
        1.5.5 Continuing evaluation which should lead to re-grouping

1.6 Developing teacher-prepared materials and/or selecting commercial materials to provide:

    1.6.1 Appropriate reading materials which are based on the reading interest and specific needs of the children

    1.6.2 Duplication of these materials and listing of selected commercial materials for purposes of teacher in-service education

1.7 Maintaining a reading resource room which serves to provide:

    1.7.1 An attractive emotional climate for these emotionally disturbed, retarded readers

    1.7.2 A resource for teachers and supervisors to develop new and different approaches in the instructional program

2. Teacher In-Service Education

2.1 Providing demonstration lessons at request of the principal

2.2 Conferring periodically with individual classroom teachers whose pupils are in the program so as to involve them as members of the team

2.3 Conferring with other teachers at the request of the principal

2.4 Participating in grade, group and/or faculty conferences

2.5 Using the reading resource room for these conferences to demonstrate techniques and procedures

2.6 Serving as liaison member between clinic staff and school

2.7 Conferring periodically with principal

3. Record Keeping

Maintaining an ongoing pupil folder containing selection data, test data, anecdotal records, speech diagnosis, conference records, etc.

4. Evaluation

4.1 Conferring periodically with the classroom teacher to ascertain pupil's functional reading level, behavioral patterns, peer relationships, etc.

4.2 Periodic evaluation of each pupil in terms of reading achievement through standardized measurements; personal-social development through clinic staff evaluation; and classroom teacher evaluation

5. Public Relations

5.1 Participating in parents' and community meetings

5.2 Inviting parents and community members to visit the reading resource room and observe the pupils at work

PUPILS REFERRED FOR SERVICE

Principal_____   Date_____

School_____

Reading Teacher_____

Name	Class	I.Q.	Current Reading Level	Reading Test	Disposition

4.2.5 SELECTING THE OFFICIAL CASELOAD

The reading clinic teacher is the person who begins the work of selecting the pupils for the official caseload. If the reading program is new to the school, the reading teacher's first responsibility is to discuss with the principal the specific criteria for selection and the necessary procedures and forms to be used. If the reading program is continued from the previous school year, she locates those boys and girls still on the reading clinic caseload. She then lists these pupils by grade, class, room number, and teacher's name. Since she has available ongoing anecdotal records and reading achievement data from the previous end-term testing, the reading teacher is now able to form tentative groups and begin her work with these pupils.

The school principal or his assistant lists the names of new candidates on the referral forms. On the facing page appears a copy of the form, "Pupils Referred for Service."

The reading clinic teacher obtains the complete school record cards for each pupil and studies them in order to eliminate anyone who obviously does not meet the criteria for selection. The names of the remaining candidates are entered separately on a "Selection Data Sheet" (see form on p. 25), together with identifying data and other needed information which may be found on the pupil's cumulative record cards, personal and educational data, health records, and test data. At this point she is ready to confer with class teachers, guidance counselors, and other school personnel who may give her pertinent information regarding the student's reading problem and behavior record.

The next step is for the reading clinic teacher to interview these boys and girls briefly, either singly or in small groups. She will meet them in the reading room in order to explain that they are being considered for membership in the reading program, to point out some of the features of this program, and to tell them that they will be called in soon for a reading test. It has been found that this type of careful orientation of the pupil makes for good motivation toward the program as well as for optimum performance on the reading test. The reading clinic teacher should select a test appropriate to the student's reading level and should adhere strictly to the directions as given in the standardized test manuals.

While the boys and girls are being tested, the reading clinic teacher observes them, inconspicuously making note of their test behavior and attitudes. Such notes are later transferred to the cover of the test booklet. Scoring is done carefully and checked a second time. For some pupils, unable to follow directions for the selected test, the reading teacher may select a simpler one or she may determine if the pupil is a non-reader by informal testing with primer or pre-primer material. (At this point in the selection procedure, further reading diagnosis is not yet essential.)

After completion of her records on the referred cases, the reading clinic teacher transmits them to the social worker with whom she may discuss the cases. Occasionally the reading test results reveal a pupil who is not sufficiently retarded to require reading help outside the classroom. In such a case the test findings are reported to the school principal or his assistant, with the explanation that no further steps to study the boy or girl will be taken by the reading clinic at the present time. The other cases are then referred to the clinic team for continuation of the intake studies. (See "The Intake Study," p. 82.) Since these clinical procedures require varying amounts of time to complete, the reading teacher has opportunity in the meantime to begin work with her provisional caseload and with the official cases remaining from the previous term.

4.2.6   THE PROVISIONAL CASELOAD

The purpose of the provisional caseload program is to afford additional service to schools while the clinicians are completing the procedures necessary for the selection of the regular caseload. The reading clinic teacher accepts students from among the upper graders who are referred by the principal. These are pupils with a reading achievement somewhat below grade level who can be excepted to profit from a short-term program. The primary goal is to bring them up to grade level.

The intake procedures for these students include a conference with the classroom teacher, an appraisal of record cards, the completion of a selection data sheet, and the measurement of reading achievement. The last includes both a standardized silent reading test and an informal reading inventory.

Reading sessions for this provisional group are also held twice weekly with groups ranging in number from seven to ten. Some of the more advanced pupils on the regular official caseload may be grouped with the "provisionals." The reading clinic teacher makes a concentrated effort to help these students to extend their reading skills, and also to develop interpretive reading power. A variety of approaches and materials are used in the lessons which are systematically planned and developed.

It has been found that most of the pupils in the provisional program are eager for reading help. Perhaps because of this strong motivation to improve and this special interest in their reading shown by the reading clinic teacher these students usually make substantial progress in a relatively short period of time. Before work is discontinued with them, they are retested with silent reading tests.

4.2.7 READING DIAGNOSIS

During the selection procedure the reading clinic teacher should carry out a partial study of each pupil which constitutes the groundwork for her reading diagnosis. She should have obtained fairly dependable grade scores from silent reading tests. In scoring and interpreting these standardized achievement tests, the reading teacher should make note of the pupil who has attempted to answer only a few items but answers them accurately. This may reveal the over-cautious boy or girl who, being afraid to make a mistake, may be underrated by the test score. This pupil apparently attempting very little may be fearful and lacking in confidence. The reading clinic teacher should bring up this matter with the clinic team to see if the social worker and the psychologist have information which is relevant to the problem. Is the pupil being handled by overly punitive methods at home? Has he a history of phobic reactions, for example, at the time of school entrance? What is the reason for his history of excessive absence from school? Are there health problems? In what particular ways can the reading teacher encourage the pupil? Did the psychologist's intake study reveal any special interests or other assets? Is this a potential "full study case," where the clinic team will provide counseling or treatment for parent and child, and where frequent consultations between instructional and clinical staff, including the psychiatrist, will be needed? Until more facts are known, the reading clinic teacher will be gentle and protective of the pupil, trying to help him to succeed in his first efforts to read before the group.

A vividly contrasting picture is suggested by the test booklet of a boy of the same age and school grade. He has marked every item on the test; and the reading teacher's notes, made at the time, show that he completed the test before the time limit had expired. His grade score is very low because most items throughout the test were marked incorrectly. Rereading her observations of his behavior during the test, she remembers his excitable behavior, his tendency to ask questions, his effort to distract other children, his breaking two pencil points, the request to leave the room. She may sigh a little as the immediate realization comes to her that this pupil will present challenges of many sorts. As to his reading, she will hope to find some areas of special interest and build a lesson plan with his participation very much in mind. She knows that it is highly probable that he will want to take the center of the reading group, initiating disruptive behavior if she does not help him to experience importance in legitimate activity. It may be true that he feels just as unhappy as the boy previously described, who was afraid to make mistakes, and is as lacking in confidence that he can learn to read, but his methods of dealing with his problems (the nature of his "defense") are entirely different. The reading clinic teacher contemplates the two boys and is not certain that she will be able to keep them in the same group. Are they too opposite? Or, will skillful planning and handling on her part finally result in the boys complementing each other so that the one tending to depression and withdrawal is stimulated and comes alive, while some of his self-control rubs off on this over-active, impulsive dynamo? Again, she decides to consult her clinic teammates, if possible before, rather than after, the class teacher begins to come to her with problems about this boy who has so few skills with which to occupy himself at school.

With both these boys and all the others who have passed through the clinic team's scrutiny (and with her selection sheets and test materials now returned to her), the reading clinic teacher will proceed to make a more technical reading diagnosis. She will want to know the actual defects and weaknesses and also the reading skills which have been learned. Some of this diagnosis will be informal, approached with attractive reading material on the pupil's probable reading level, and hopefully aimed at bringing out his best effort to read. Afterwards, the reading clinic teacher can use more formal oral test material, such as one of Gray's Oral Reading Paragraphs and, routinely, the Roswell-Chall Diagnostic Test of Word Analysis Skills. Graded word lists are also employed to determine the level at which a pupil can recognize words at sight; and these lists can provide information regarding his competence in word-attack skills. Results of all this individual oral testing of each pupil will be recorded on a copy of "An Analysis of Reading Difficulties" which appears on the pages immediately following. By checking these analysis sheets while observing his efforts to read selected material during the administration of an informal reading inventory, the reading teacher can make an appraisal of a student's functional level in reading as well as determine his specific reading needs. Such testing is repeated, with appropriate notations entered on this analysis form, not less than three times a year.

The informal reading inventory (I.R.I.) is an informal diagnostic tool used to determine the student's strengths and limitations in word analysis and comprehension skills, and his level of reading ability. A teacher or

AN ANALYSIS OF READING DIFFICULTIES

Name _____Class_____School_____

Date Date Date Date Date

1. **Limited vocabulary**

2. **Substitutions**

3. **Reversals**

4. **Insertions**

5. **Repetitions**

6. **Omissions**

7. **Vocalization**

8. **Word attack skills**

   8.1   Initial consonants

   8.2   Final consonants

   8.3   Word endings

   8.4   Consonant digraphs

   8.5   Vowel digraphs

   8.6   Diphthongs

   8.7   Consonant blends

   8.8   Vowels

      8.8.1 Medial vowels

      8.8.2 Long vowels

      8.8.3 Short vowels

   8.9   Overdependence on illustrations

   8.10 Inability to fuse phonetic elements

   8.11 Spells out words

9. **Phrasing**

   9.1   Word by word

   9.2   Punctuation ignored

   9.3   Incorrect word groupings

10. **Visual analysis**

      Dependent on:

   10.1 General configuration

   10.2 Initial parts

   10.3 Striking features

11. **Comprehension skills**

   11.1 Understanding the main thought of:
   11.1.1 a sentence
   11.1.2 a paragraph
   11.1.3 a selection

   11.2 Reading to gain and retain information through:
   11.2.1 recall of significant details
   11.2.2 determining sequence
   11.2.3 developing an outline and summary

   11.3 Reading to discover relationship by:
   11.2.1 classifying information
   11.3.2 following directions
   11.3.3 combining ideas from more than one source (upper grades)

   11.4 Reading to develop ability:
   11.4.1 to predict outcomes
   11.4.2 to draw inferences
   11.4.3 to form opinions

12. **Voice**

   12.1 Monotone

   12.2 Too loud

   12.3 Too low and indistinct

   12.4 High pitched

13. **Speech difficulties**

   13.1 Enunciation

   13.2 Mispronunciation

   13.3 Speech defects

14. **Emotional—Social—Personal**

   14.1 Timid

   14.2 Anxious

   14.3 Lacks confidence

   14.4 Reads with false confidence

   14.5 Resists help

   14.6 Hyperactive—short attention span

   14.7 Demands inordinate amount of attention

   14.8 Indifferent—lethargic

   14.9 Does not relate well to group

   14.10 Does not relate well to reading teacher

   14.11 Evidences qualities of leadership

   14.12 Lacks initiative

Additional Comments

group of teachers may develop the informal reading inventory. Material should be selected from a set of graded readers. The student is asked to read one passage orally and a second passage silently. In selecting the material for the student to read the teacher is guided by the student's recorded standardized test score. The teacher determines the pupil's instructional level by administering this informal reading inventory, noting down errors in phonic analysis, word recognition and comprehension. She is thus able to determine specific instructional needs. She observes the pupil's attitude toward reading and evidences of physical defects. The skillful teacher makes careful observations of the pupil in this reading situation.

Books are shared by the instructional staff members, as are school-duplicated poems, other materials, and exercises for developing word-analysis and comprehension skills. The most effective exercise material has been found to be that which is closely related to some reading need which has just arisen within the group. Word-analysis and vocabulary study is most likely to be retained if the initial focus of attention is on a word in a selection which has been read.

It will be noted that the reading clinic teacher is directive in her approach to the reading group. This is so because pupils with a deep sense of failure in regard to school work, who also have many other behavior problems, do not readily form a group—no matter how small it is. If they are "ready" for reading help, they are likely to be individually demanding of the reading teacher's time and attention, and also actively resentful or competitive with the others who are assigned to be with her at the same hour. It is only by demonstrating instructional and guidance skills of a high order that the reading clinic teacher forms a group of these diverse individuals. At first, they tend to rush to the reading room alone, and, hopefully, ahead of their group members in order to be first with the reading teacher. Only after some weeks or months of experience do they show signs of interest in each other and sometimes appear smilingly together in pairs, or in a larger group, with an eager question or request. At this stage, the reading teacher finds that she is not the sole source of enthusiasm and of ideas; the boys and girls themselves begin to bring in materials, questions, and suggestions which can be incorporated in the reading teacher's plans for the group.

It is thought that this emergence of a successful reading group constitutes the vital force accounting for the increased learning which occurs with the great majority of these pupils. They are accepted, first by the reading teacher and eventually by the other boys and girls for what they are—poor readers, hoping to improve. There is safety in the group where all share a common problem; they reduce the need to evade or deny their reading difficulty. They benefit sometimes even by listening to some phase of instruction directed especially at another pupil, when they themselves do not need this particular exercise. Perhaps it is helpful for boys and girls who so frequently are merely on the fringe of understanding what goes on in a classroom, to experience overlearning at times, and to be able to say to themselves, "I already know that; he is having the trouble I used to have." The major motivation for each pupil to work harder and to learn to read should come about as a result of the stimulus derived from interaction in the group. Of course, to the extent that the parent-child relationships are also improving as the result of the clinic team's work, the child's outlook on arrival at school should become more optimistic and this change should also contribute to learning.

Whenever a disturbed pupil persistently resists becoming a cooperative member of a group, and prevents the other pupils from learning, the reading clinic teacher should take steps to change this situation. Sometimes a few short periods of individual work—partially teaching and partially counseling him with regard to his unacceptable behavior in the group—will effect a changed attitude, and the pupil can be returned to his group or assigned to another. If not, other forms of study and treatment can be considered in a case conference with the clinic team.

4.2.8 MATERIALS OF INSTRUCTION

In the reading clinic many varied instructional materials should be used. These include: teacher-prepared ditto materials, experience charts, trade books and workbooks on different levels and in a great variety of curriculum and interest areas. Magazines are a valuable resource and serve to provide the pupils with pictures and "ideas." These should be used in the development of phonic skills, vocabulary enrichment and comprehension skills.

The trade books are eye-catching, attractively illustrated books, ordered from library and textbook listings and from other sources. Children's magazines can be obtained in the same way. Boys and girls should be encouraged to borrow books from the reading room for school and home use. However, resistance should not be met with insistence. Ultimately, the pupil, of his own accord, will become a book borrower. When the supply of books on a topic of great interest to any pupil is found to be insufficient, the reading clinic teacher should bring in additional materials of instruction, on the appropriate reading level, from her local library and from other sources.

Reading games—commercial, as well as those adapted or devised by the reading clinic teacher—are used to meet the pupil's specific diagnosed reading needs. Devices and materials to reinforce reading skills should be developed with the pupils. Some should be compiled into booklets; some should be developed into charts with pockets to facilitate greater variety and extended use; some should be developed into pockets of cards which may be added to from time to time. These can be referred to easily, independently on the pupil's part or used with a group. (See samples of teacher-prepared materials in Appendix D.)

Pupils' interests should be explored so that the reading clinic teacher may provide reading materials that will motivate the pupil and make him want to read. Materials, such as pictures illustrating current topics, brief newspaper clippings, cartoons, and jokes, should be displayed on bulletin boards or blackboards to awaken and develop new interests. Displays on tables or shelves which are labeled and contain reading material should be varied, such as stamp collections, foreign coins, models of cars, planes, and boats, science experiments, rock and other nature collections. If the questions "how" and "why" should follow, we should build and further develop these interests by leading the pupil to books on the subject or to other appropriate reading material.

Arts and craft materials, audio-visual aids, and puppetry are some other means of providing experiences around which reading lessons can be built. They should help pupils to shed their inhibitions and provide the setting and opportunity for some creative effort.

4.2.9 RECORD KEEPING BY THE INSTRUCTIONAL STAFF

Lesson Plans

Careful records are an important part of the reading clinic teacher's work. They should be of different types and serve many purposes. Reference has already been made to the *lesson plans* which each reading clinic teacher develops. These should be dated and filed in chronological order. There should be included a listing of the names of the pupils in each of her various groups. The lesson plans should be accessible to the Director and any other supervisor and should also be made available to newly assigned staff members in connection with their orientation to this program.

The Pupil Folder—Instructional

The pupils' folders have been briefly described earlier and will be taken up in detail here. These should be sturdy legal size folders, each with a typed label giving a pupil's name, his grade and class, his school, and the initials of his reading clinic teacher. The folder should be placed alphabetically in the reading teacher's file in the clinic office. The contents of the folder should be kept in the following order:

The Selection Data Sheet. This form contains identifying data and also statements regarding referral problems and other notations made by the reading clinic teacher and the clinicians during the selection process. (A copy of this form appears on page 25.)

A Report from the Speech Improvement Teacher. Each pupil's speech should be evaluated by the speech teacher and a written report forwarded to the reading teacher. These are usually briefly stated diagnoses of any actual defects or descriptions of poor speech habits. Recommendations for treatment should also be included. The reading clinic teacher should note the day and hour, if possible, when the pupil attends speech instruction, in order to avoid conflicts of scheduling.

An Analysis of Reading Difficulties. (A copy of this form appears on page 51.) Its use is described in the section, "Reading Diagnosis," in this chapter.

Reading Tests previously administered to the child by the reading clinic teacher. The tests used for the original measurement of reading achievement, those given for diagnostic purposes, and those used for evaluation of reading progress should all be retained and filed in the pupil's folder. Scores should be noted on a summary sheet stapled to the inside cover of the folder. The reason for retaining the actual booklet is that the reading clinic teacher should refer back to the pupil's work on a standardized test in order to check the specific nature of his difficulties. The summary form, "Record of Reading Tests," appears on the facing page.

Anecdotal Records. What a student does today gains significance in connection with what he has done previously. Therefore, the continuous anecdotal record of each pupil should be kept by the reading clinic teacher. This is of great importance to both the reading teacher and clinicians.

RECORD OF READING TESTS

Name..

Date service began..

School..

Date discharged..

graduated..

Reading Teacher 1..

2..

3..

Date 1................................

2................................

3................................

Date of Test	Class	Title of Test	Form	Score	Accuracy (if any)	Name of Examiner	Comments

Under each date when the pupil comes for instruction, the reading clinic teacher should record any significant aspect of his response to the planned lesson. She should also record statements or behavior episodes of the pupil which reflect reading growth, special difficulties in learning, and positive or negative attitudes toward himself and to his school or home situation. If she takes action with regard to a pupil's expressed need, the reading clinic teacher should be expected to make note of this also. Absences for scheduled sessions in the reading room and reasons for the absences should be noted in chronological order in the anecdotal record.

The reading clinic teacher should write summaries of all conferences held with the class teacher, the principal, and other school personnel and should include them in the anecdotal record. Summaries of conferences with the clinic team should also be placed in this pupil folder. These conferences are recorded on a special form, a duplicate of which should be filed in the clinician's confidential folder. See form, "Record of Case Conference," which appears on the facing pages.

The reading clinic teacher's folders should remain in the office in order to be available for consultation by the clinicians concerned with the same pupils. Having the pupil's folder for study prior to a case conference with the reading clinic teacher facilitates understanding by the team of the nature of the problem. The psychologist and social worker should also study their own clinical material for the purpose of finding tentative answers to questions or of posing further questions to themselves which need more detailed study. If the reading clinic teacher also has reviewed her own anecdotal records prior to the case conference, the entire team would be better prepared to think about the pupil in objective terms and to reach agreement as to necessary changes in the handling of the case by any or all of the staff members who are concerned.

Caseload Record

The reading clinic teacher should maintain an ongoing list of the pupils in her caseload. She should complete the data as regards name, date of birth, class, intelligence test, speech diagnosis, and achievement test in reading—original and subsequent tests. Other columns should be maintained by the clinical personnel. On page 60 appears the form, "Caseload Record."

RECORD OF CASE CONFERENCE

_____School_____Referred by_____
    Name of Child   Name   Title

Date Scheduled_____Place_____

Attended by: Reading Teacher_____Social Worker_____Psychologist_____
    Others_____

Reason for Referral

Other Problems

Discussion

Plans

Reported by_____

CASELOAD RECORD

School Year _____

Names of Pupils	Reading Teacher	Date of Birth	Class	Date Service Began	Group Intelligence Test	Stanford-Binet WISC	Psychological Service	Social Work Service	Psychiatric Service	Pediatric Examination	Eye Examination	Speech Diagnosis and Treatment	Ach. Test in Reading ORIGINAL I II III	Ach. Test in Reading JUNE____ I II III	Ach. Test in Reading JUNE____ I II III	Orig-inal Retard-ation	Read-Gain	Cum. Read. Gains Based on Orig. Test Scores	Comments

Names of **Classroom Teachers – Class**

Code
D – Diagnosis
C – Consultation and/or Conference
T – Treatment
I – Parent Interview

Accuracy Ratings
VH – Very High
H – High
M – Medium
L – Low
VL – Very Low

4.2.10 STAFF DEVELOPMENT PROGRAMS
FOR THE INSTRUCTIONAL STAFF

The reading clinic program should be designed to provide a careful orientation for the reading clinic teacher, as well as an ongoing program for staff growth. It is necessary to plan meetings and conferences that will continue to provide stimulation and opportunity for upgrading instruction, developing increased understanding of the dynamics of behavior, diagnosis, and test interpretation.

It may be well to invite outstanding authorities to address the staff at general conferences. These conferences should occur not less than four times a year. The raising of questions, the sharing of mutual thinking and experiences should be part of such meetings. The staff should attend and/or participate in professional conferences and conventions.

The Director should maintain a professional library containing texts, yearbooks, journals, and other publications in reading. The staff should be encouraged to utilize and keep abreast of these readings. They should be kept apprised of the courses being offered in the nearby colleges and schools and should be urged to enroll.

Observations of the instructional program by the supervisor should be followed by an individual conference with the reading teacher to discuss the highlights of the lesson and mutually agreed upon suggestions for improvement. The underlying goal for all these procedures should be to provide the staff with mutual stimulation and opportunities for growth.

4.2.11 IN-SERVICE TEACHER EDUCATION

The staff of a reading clinic has the responsibility to diagnose the reading difficulty of the boys and girls referred, to evaluate the diagnosis and then plan a program to correct these reading disabilities, to provide an ongoing program for these students both instructionally and clinically and to provide clinical services for their families. The reading clinic teacher serves as the liaison with the pupil's class teacher or English teacher or other assigned teacher and meets with her twice a month to exchange and share information about the student.

The staff of a reading clinic also has the responsibility of sharing their knowledge of the teaching of reading with other members of the school staff. This may be done through clinic staff participation in individual conferences with teachers, in grade, group, and/or faculty conference.

The reading clinic teacher may demonstrate techniques and devices; she may have teachers observe the instructional program; give demonstration lessons; classroom teachers may visit the reading resource room which should contain many suggested practices and procedures.

The reading clinic teacher should maintain a record of these sessions held to assist teachers. Included in this record should also be the conferences held with principals or supervisors to plan these sessions and in some situations the conferences held with the superintendent when a district-wide in-service education program is planned; and records of conferences held with other school personnel.

On the facing page appears the form, "Record of In-Service Teacher Education."

4.3   THE CLINICAL PROGRAM

4.3.1   PERSONNEL

The clinic should be staffed with a clinic team. The team should be comprised of a psychologist and a social worker, assigned on a full time basis, and a psychiatrist who serves not less than one half-day a week in the clinic.

4.3.2   THE WORK OF THE SOCIAL WORKER

The work of the social worker should cover a broad range of functions, for she or he has the responsibility of integrating the various clinical services. The social worker's major responsibility should be service to parents. Of prime importance is the work of interviewing the parents or guardians of all the boys and girls considered for the program, since one of the criteria for the pupil's acceptance is parental willingness to become involved. It is the assessment of the parents' motivation for help and capacity to use it that determines, in a large measure, the type of service to be provided.

If at the intake phase, the social worker should find that the services of another agency are more appropriate, it is advisable that the parents be helped to recognize this. The social worker then should take the initiative in making the referral. If another agency is already involved in a

RECORD OF IN-SERVICE TEACHER EDUCATION

Month_____19____

School_____

Staff Member_____

Classroom Teacher–Date	Grade–Date	Group–Date	Faculty–Date	Principal–Date	Supt.–Date	Demon.–Date	Use of Reading–Resource Room–Date	Meetings With Other School Personnel

family situation, the social worker should clarify the roles and functions and work out a cooperative relationship with the other organization. In this way the services of the reading clinic can be coordinated with those provided by other community agencies.

The social worker should share clinical responsibility for intake with the psychologist, who makes a diagnostic study of the pupil. In this reading clinic setting, the focus in the initial interview with the parents should be on the educational development of the child and siblings, and the parents' feelings about the child's learning difficulty. Thus, the mother can be encouraged to give information which seems important to her, and need not feel pressed in the first interview for details of family history which she may not see as relevant at this time. The way will then be left open for the parents to come back to see the social worker again. One aim of the social worker should be to establish good rapport with the parents in a relationship based on helpful understanding of the problems sometimes revealed by the parents. At the conclusion of the intake studies, the parents may be accepted for treatment, or for counseling service, depending upon the need, readiness and accessibility for help.

In a team relationship with the psychologist and reading teacher, the social worker should participate in a continuing evaluation of child-parent relationships and of the many aspects of the environment which may handicap or favor the child. The social worker should share responsibility with the psychologist and psychiatrist for full studies leading to diagnosis and treatment. A full study should be preceded by several interviews between the social worker and the mother in order to clarify the problem and secure as much understanding as possible. The social worker should prepare the mother for the diagnostic interview of mother and child by the psychiatrist.

The social worker should plan and participate in clinic conferences. Many of these conferences involve only the social worker and the psychologist. In all full study cases, however, the social worker, psychologist, and psychiatrist should take part in the clinical conference. The case conference on the individual pupil calls for joint planning by both clinical and instructional workers. The case conference may also include classroom teachers, principals, other school personnel, and social workers from community agencies. The social worker should make note of all recommendations requiring environmental changes and wherever possible follow through in their implementation. She should confer with the school nurse and plan for the medical examination of every pupil in the program and an ophthalmological and/or optometric examination. The social worker should strive to help parents utilize, for the benefit of their children, educational and recreational services present in their community.

It is the responsibility of the social worker to set up for each pupil the clinical record to which all members of the team are to contribute. On the following pages appear a detailed account of the work opportunities and responsibilities of the social worker, "Job Analysis of the Social Worker," and the forms, "Social Worker's Schedule" and "Social Worker's Numerical Summary of Case Contacts."

JOB ANALYSIS OF THE SOCIAL WORKER

1. *Selection of Pupils*

   1.1 The social worker confers with the reading clinic teacher and with the psychologist concerning:

   1.1.1 the boys and girls referred for clinical screening (following the reading clinic teacher's testing and evaluation) to determine which individuals are to be given psychological evaluation prior to initial activity by the social worker

   1.1.2 the disposition of pupils who have been processed and approved for service by clinical and instructional staff

   1.2 An initial interview with the parents is held by the social worker to establish eligibility, to involve the parents actively, and to secure the parents' written consent for service.

   1.3 The social worker refers parents to an outside agency when this is indicated.

   1.4 The social worker confers with the psychologist and at times with the psychiatrist regarding intake.

   1.5 The case record is set up after the social worker clears the case with Social Service Exchange, if such clearing house agency is available, and then records intake interview.

   1.6 The social worker confers on "clinic day" with the psychologist and the reading clinic teacher to help in understanding the needs of the individual child and his family problems.

2. *Continued Contact with Parents*

   2.1 The social worker interviews the parents to obtain medical history and from time to time to inform parents of progress and of particular needs and problems.

   2.2 The social worker arranges the medical examination which is held in the pupil's school. The parents are always present for this examination and the social worker is often present.

2.3 The social worker arranges for an ophthalmological and/or optometric examination.

2.4 Where there is indication of the need for further study because of a pupil's behavior ,or failure to achieve, the social worker arranges a series of interviews with the parents in order to obtain further understanding of the family problems and to prepare the parents for a diagnostic evaluation by the psychiatrist.

2.5 The social worker confers with the psychologist and the psychiatrist following the diagnostic interview. The social worker helps the parents to carry out recommendations made as a result of the three-way conference.

3. *Treatment and Counseling of Parents*

3.1 Selected parents are offered weekly appointments with the social worker to help work out problems which affect the child's learning and social adjustments.

3.2 Parents needing less intensive service are seen once or twice a month.

3.3 The social worker plans workshops with parents concerned with group discussions of common problems of parents and children.

4. *School Conferences*

As the need arises, case conferences of the reading clinic personnel are held with class teachers and supervisors regarding pupils serviced by the clinic.

5. *Cooperation with Other School Personnel*

The social worker participates with other members of the staff in meetings arranged with school principals, class teachers, or other school personnel, relative to this program.

6. *Cooperation with Supervisory Staff*

6.1 The social worker attends general staff meetings called by the Director of the reading clinic.

6.2 The Director sets up a schedule of conferences with the social worker in order to discuss the program and any problems connected with the social worker's work.

6.3 The social worker follows plans worked out cooperatively with the Director regarding hours of work and schedule of activities;

SOCIAL WORKER'S SCHEDULE

Social Worker_____   Week of_____19_____

Day		Appointments	Conferences	Psychiatric Appointments
Mon.	8:30			
	9:00			
	10:00			
	11:00			
	1:00			
	2:00			
	3:00			
Tues.	8:30			
	9:00			
	10:00			
	11:00			
	1:00			
	2:00			
	3:00			
Wed.	8:30			
	9:00			
	10:00			
	11:00			
	1:00			
	2:00			
	3:00			
Thur.	8:30			
	9:00			
	10:00			
	11:00			
	1:00			
	2:00			
	3:00			
Fri.	8:30			
	9:00			
	10:00			
	11:00			
	1:00			
	2:00			
	3:00			

SOCIAL WORKER'S NUMERICAL SUMMARY OF CASE CONTACTS

Social Worker_____School_____Week of_____19_____

	Current Week	Carried Forward	New Totals
1. Intake			
1.1 Initial			
1.2 Continued			
1.3 Appointments: Broken—Cancelled			
1.4 Number Rejected			
2. Diagnostic Studies After Intake			
2.1 Partial Study—Number of Parents			
2.1.1 Number of Interviews			
2.2 Full Study—Number of Parents			
2.2.1 Number of Interviews			
3. Treatment			
3.1 Social Worker Only			
3.1.1 Number of Parents			
3.1.2 Number of Interviews			
3.2 After Psychiatric Examination			
3.2.1 Number of Parents			
3.2.2 Number of Interviews			
3.2.3 Number of Pupils			
3.2.4 Number of Interviews			
4. Parent Groups			
5. Agency Contact and Reports			
6. Conferences			
6.1 Reading Teacher			
6.2 Classroom Teacher			
6.3 Other School Personnel			
6.4 Psychologist			
6.5 Psychiatrist			
6.6 Full Team			
6.7 General Staff			
6.8 Clinic Staff			
6.9 Others			
7. Recording: Names of Cases			

at the conclusion of each week an amended or corrected record of what was accomplished is submitted along with a weekly numerical summary of case contacts.

6.4 It is the responsibility of the social worker to provide statistical data and to assist in the drawing up of year-end reports.

7. Cooperation with Community Agencies

7.1 The social worker works cooperatively with community agencies in making referrals of children or parents who need service which is not available through the reading clinic, such as securing camp and institutional placements.

7.2 The social worker interprets the clinic to the community social workers when there is need for it.

4.3.3 THE WORK OF THE PSYCHOLOGIST

The psychologist in the reading clinic program is involved in selection, orientation, initial psychological appraisal, diagnostic evaluation, and full study of the pupil and his difficulties. In addition, the psychologist sees selected pupils on a regular basis for counseling or treatment and, under certain conditions, may carry on research which is relevant to the program. The work of the psychologist may vary in emphasis on one or another aspect of these clinical functions, according to the needs of the boys and girls.

The psychologist works in a close day-to-day relationship with the social worker and, as a member of the full clinical team including the psychiatrist, participates in diagnostic and treatment conferences. The psychologist and social worker meet on "clinic day" with the reading clinic teacher for scheduled case conferences.

The psychologist is expected to provide treatment for pupils with special problems either by direct supportive counseling or, depending on the pupil's need, by more intensive therapy. Both individual and group treatment methods are utilized based on what is appropriate for the pupil concerned. Treatment plans for the pupils should be made in agreement with the social worker and psychiatrist. General policy requires that only children whose parents are also receiving treatment on a regular basis from the social worker should be accepted for treatment by the psychologist.

On the following pages appears a detailed account of the work opportunities and responsibilities of the psychologist, the "Job Analysis of the Psychologist" and the forms, "Psychologist's Weekly Schedule" and "Psychologist's Numerical Summary of Case Contacts."

PSYCHOLOGIST'S WEEKLY SCHEDULE

Week of..

Psychologist's Name..

Day	School	Pupils*	Conference	Other Work
MON				
TUES				
WED				
THURS				
FRI				

*(T) = Therapy   (D) = Diagnostic Study

JOB ANALYSIS OF THE PSYCHOLOGIST

1. *Selection of Pupils*

   1.1 The psychologist plans with the reading clinic teacher and the social worker concerning:

   1.1.1 the priority of cases to be studied

   1.1.2 the question of whether certain referred pupils meet the selection criteria

   1.2 An individual intelligence examination is administered by the psychologist in doubtful cases prior to the social worker's interview of the parents.

   1.3 An initial psychological study with a battery of projective tests is administered by the psychologist after a direct interview with the pupil.

   1.4 The psychologist holds clinical intake conferences with the social worker and, in certain cases, with the psychiatrist.

   1.5 The psychologist participates in scheduled "clinic day" conferences with the social worker and the reading clinic teacher regarding clinical findings which have a bearing on the approach to the pupil in the reading room.

   1.6 The psychologist records numerical data on statistical cards and prepares reports for the confidential case record. (See "Psychologist's Statistical Record Form" on pp. 96 and 97.)

2. *Further Diagnostic Evaluation of Selected Pupils*

   2.1 Selected cases are referred to the psychologist by the reading clinic teacher, the social worker or other school personnel because of special problems, e.g., failure to respond to the instructional program, disruptive behavior in the classroom, maladjustment at home, etc.

   2.2 The psychologist studies the pupil's confidential record and the anecdotal record kept by the reading clinic teacher.

   2.3 An individual psychological examination, the procedure depending upon the nature of the case but usually including a WISC or Stanford-Binet, a Rorschach, and other projective tests appropriate to the individual case are administered by the psychologist.

   2.4 The psychologist consults with the social worker as to whether referral for psychiatric examination is indicated.

2.5 In cases of full study including psychiatric examination, a conference of the clinic team is held to arrive at a diagnosis and to consider possible changes in the approach to parents and child.

2.6 A conference of the clinic team and the reading clinic teacher is held to clarify the underlying dynamics affecting the pupil's learning and behavior.

3. *Treatment and Counseling of Pupils*

3.1 After full clinical study of a pupil and with approval of the social worker and the psychiatrist, the psychologist may arrange to work with a pupil on a regular weekly treatment basis.

3.2 The psychologist also gives counseling service to boys and girls who have not had full study but who are in need of supportive help in an individual situation.

3.3 With the approval of the psychiatrist, the psychologist may work with selected pupils in therapy groups.

4. *School Conferences*

As the need arises, the reading clinic personnel holds case conferences with class teachers and supervisors, regarding boys and girls serviced by the clinic.

5. *Cooperation with Other School Personnel*

The psychologist participates with other members of the staff in meetings arranged with school principals, class teachers, or other school personnel, relative to the program.

6. *Cooperation with Supervisory Staff*

6.1 The psychologist attends staff meetings called by the Director of the reading clinic.

6.2 The Director sets up a schedule of conferences with the psychologist in order to discuss the program and any problems connected with the psychologist's work.

6.3 The psychologist follows plans worked out cooperatively with the Director regarding hours of work and schedule of activities; at the conclusion of each week an amended or corrected record of what was accomplished is submitted along with a weekly numerical summary of case contacts.

6.4 It is the responsibility of the psychologist to provide statistical data and assist in the drawing up of year-end reports.

7. Research

The psychologist may participate in special plans for approved research in the area of reading disability; he may also help set up a special research project for doctoral dissertation.

PSYCHOLOGIST'S NUMERICAL SUMMARY OF CASE CONTACTS

Psychologist_____Week of_____

	Current Week	Carried Forward	New Totals
1. Contacts with or about pupils			
1.1 Diagnostic contacts with pupils			
1.2 Continuous contact interviews with pupils			
1.3 Parental interviews			
1.4 Conferences with other reading clinic members			
1.5 Conferences with other school personnel			
1.6 Group tests			
1.7 Others:_____			

	New in Current Week	Carried Forward	Totals
2. Number of pupils who have received:			
2.1 Individual diagnostic study			
2.2 Individual treatment			
2.3 Individual counseling			
2.4 Group psychotherapy			
3. Number of Groups			

4.3.4   THE WORK OF THE PSYCHIATRIST

The school psychiatrist in the reading clinic has the responsibility for the psychiatric diagnosis of the pupils referred for full study. He can make recommendations to the social worker and psychologist as to the type of treatment needed. He may also carry selected boys and girls in treatment, or make recommendations for referral to other agencies.

Another important function of the psychiatrist should be to serve as consultant to the psychologist and social worker on cases with which he himself is not directly involved. The psychiatrist should also participate in conferences with the reading teacher on the mental hygiene aspects of their work, as well as on the handling of individuals in the reading groups. On the following pages appears a detailed account of the work opportunities and responsibilities of the psychiatrist, "Job Analysis of the Psychiatrist," and the form, "Psychiatrist's Monthly Work Sheet."

JOB ANALYSIS OF THE PSYCHIATRIST

1. *Diagnosis and Evaluation*

   1.1 The psychiatrist conducts psychiatric interview sessions with parents and children.
   1.2 The psychiatrist holds clinical conferences on selected cases with the social worker and the psychologist.
   1.3 On the basis of these sessions and conferences the psychiatrist arrives at a diagnosis and evaluation for selected cases and helps determine the course of treatment.

2. *Treatment*

   2.1 The psychiatrist takes on for treatment those cases, parents and/or children, who need such help.
   2.2 The psychiatrist supervises both social worker and psychologist in carrying out treatment for designated cases.

PSYCHIATRIST'S MONTHLY WORK SHEET

Name_____   Month_____ 19____

Name of Pupil	Int. with* Pupil	Family* Int.	Treatment* Pupil	Parent	Groups	Agency	Initial Conference	Case Conf.	School Personnel	Broken Appts.
Total										

*Indicate date

3. *Consultation Services*

The psychiatrist is available, on a limited basis, for consultation with reading clinic personnel, other school personnel, and parents.

4. *Record Keeping*

4.1 The psychiatrist records his findings for the confidential case records.

4.2 The psychiatrist corresponds with community agencies when he deems it necessary.

4.3 The psychiatrist confers with the Director of the reading clinic regarding the cases he is working with.

4.4 The psychiatrist sets up a weekly plan of sessions and conferences.

4.3.5 THE WORK OF THE CLINICAL SUPERVISORS

In those clinic programs where the staff in the different disciplines is increased to the point where supervision of the separate disciplines is essential, supervisors will be needed. Their roles require definition. Some of the work of these supervisors of separate disciplines can be readily adapted to suit the needs of smaller school systems.

The social worker and psychologist serving as supervisors should have both administrative and supervisory functions. With the Director, they participate in conferences pertaining to the effective functioning of the clinical staff. They also should take part in the orientation program for all new staff members, help in planning general and special staff meetings, prepare annual and other reports about the clinical aspects of this work, and in general strive to support policies which carry out mental hygiene principles.

All new clinical workers are given a week of orientation and are assigned temporarily to the headquarter's clinic for this purpose. This provides for a period of working under close supervision. These new clinicians are also included in the orientation provided for the new instructional staff members. In this way the integration of these different disciplines becomes an essential aspect of their introduction to the program as a whole.

4.3.6 THE SUPERVISING SOCIAL WORKER

The supervising social worker is responsible for the social work staff. A new member of the staff regardless of length of experience should be given supervisory conference time, following orientation, on a regular bi-weekly basis. Senior caseworkers should have scheduled consultations, usually on a monthly basis.

In advance of each week every social worker submits a weekly schedule. At the conclusion of the week each social worker submits a revised schedule of the past week showing the activities accomplished. Accompanying this revised schedule is a completed statistical sheet. It is the responsibility of the supervisor to analyze these forms each week.

Social workers' meetings are held once a month. The planning of these meetings is the responsibility of a committee of social workers in cooperation with the Supervising Social Worker and the Director. On the following pages appears a detailed account of the work opportunities and responsibilities of the Supervising Social Worker, "Job Analysis of the Supervising Social Worker."

JOB ANALYSIS OF THE
SUPERVISING SOCIAL WORKER

1. *Administrative Aspects*

   1.1 Assist the Director of the reading clinic and the Supervising Psychologist in formulating policies for the continuous integration of the clinical and instructional program.

   1.2 Assume responsibility in consultation with the Director for the social work program as it is planned and carried out in the reading clinic.

   1.3 Plan with the Director the assignment of social workers.

   1.4 Requisition books and supplies as needed for the social workers; distribute these and maintain an inventory.

   1.5 Encourage the continuous utilization of the professional library by the social worker.

   1.6 Analyze and evaluate the schedules and numerical summaries submitted by the social workers each week. Provide summary reports of the work of the social workers for interim and annual reports of the Director.

1.7 Plan with the cooperation of the social workers and the Director the programs for the monthly meetings. These should provide opportunity to share information on new techniques, publications and research, and "hard core" cases. And, at different times there should be presentations by outstanding authorities.

1.8 Participate in meetings with the Director and the public health personnel to plan a program of medical examinations for the children.

1.9 Assist the Director in setting up the schedule of the psychiatrists.

2. *In-Service Education*

2.1 Orientation of New Staff—(both instructional and clinical)

    2.1.1 Consult with the Director and with the Supervising Psychologist in planning meetings for the orientation of new staff members in all disciplines. At these meetings the Supervising Social Worker explains the role of the social worker in a reading clinic. Cases are presented which illustrate the team relationship of the social worker, psychologist, and reading clinic teacher.

2.2 Orientation of New Social Workers

    2.2.1 Social workers participate in meetings arranged for all new staff members.

    2.2.2 New social workers are assigned to the office of the Supervising Social Worker where close supervision can be provided. One goal of the orientation program is to increase the competence of the social worker in the various phases of social work as outlined in the "Job Analysis of the Social Worker." The supervisor also makes available for study the case records, annual reports, and selected references.

3. *Supervision and Consultation*

3.1 Newly assigned social workers are scheduled for supervisory conferences every other week during the first year. Senior social workers have consultation sessions once a month.

3.2 At regular intervals the supervisor and social worker check and analyze case records together.

4. *Recruitment of Social Workers*

The Director and the supervisor engage in recruitment to seek out qualified personnel. Applicants are interviewed and given an opportunity to visit the clinic.

5. *Evaluations*

> The Supervising Social Worker should evaluate and analyze the work of each new social worker at the conclusion of the year. A written evaluation drawn up in consultation with the Director is submitted. The supervisor analyzes the work of the senior case workers and makes a written evaluation each year. The latter evaluation is developed cooperatively by supervisor and social workers.

4.3.7 THE SUPERVISING PSYCHOLOGIST

The Supervising Psychologist with the approval of the Director should assign psychologists and should be responsible for all psychological work carried out in the reading clinic. The Supervising Psychologist is responsible for analyzing and checking the reports of the psychologist.

Supervision of each psychologist should be planned in accordance with the nature and extent of training as well as experience. During the first year, a psychologist should meet with the supervisor every two weeks. Senior psychologists usually request and should be given consultation time about once a month to discuss the progress of the work and the particular problems with which they are concerned.

Staff development should be a continuing objective of the supervisor. The planning of psychologists' meetings, which should be held every month, should be the responsibility of a committee in cooperation with the supervisor and the Director. Group consultation on difficult cases, discussion of newer approaches to psychological diagnosis and treatment, and the sharing of experiences which have been found to improve communication with other clinical and instructional staff members are some of the suggested topics to be discussed at these staff meetings.

The work of the Supervising Psychologist also includes helping the psychologists plan and coordinate their research undertakings on children with reading disability, in accordance with the requirements of their school systems, and of the colleges approving their theses. On the following pages appears a detailed account of the work opportunities and responsibilities of the Supervising Psychologist, the "Job Analysis of the Supervising Psychologist."

JOB ANALYSIS OF THE SUPERVISING PSYCHOLOGIST

1. *Administrative Aspects*

   1.1 Assist the Director of the reading clinic and the Supervising Social Worker in formulating policies for the continuous integration of the clinical and instructional program.

   1.2 Assume responsibility in consultation with the Director for the psychological work as it is planned and carried out in the reading clinic.

   1.3 Assign psychologists with the approval of the Director.

   1.4 Requisition psychological equipment and supplies as needed by psychologists in the reading clinics. Assume responsibility for providing and distributing necessary psychological supplies and for keeping an inventory of these materials.

   1.5 Analyze and evaluate weekly schedules of psychologists and numerical summaries of case contacts. Provide summary reports of the work of psychologists for interim and annual reports of the Director.

   1.6 Plan with the cooperation of the other psychologists programs for monthly meetings of the group. These should provide opportunity to share information on new techniques and publications, relevant research, differential diagnosis of difficult cases. At different times there should be presentations by outstanding authorities.

2. *In-Service Education*

   2.1 Orientation of New Staff Members (both instructional and clinical)
      2.1.1 Participation with the Director and the Supervising Social Worker in planning meetings and leading discussions on such topics as:
         factors associated with reading disability in "hard core" reading disability cases and the resources of the reading clinic for handling such cases;
         the work of the reading clinic psychologist, with illustrative case accounts of the retarded readers.

   2.2 Orientation of New Psychologists
      2.2.1 Psychologists participate in meetings arranged for all new staff members.

2.2.2 Psychologists work in close contact with the supervisor before being given a particular assignment. One goal of the orientation program is to increase the competence of the psychologist in the various phases of psychological work as outlined in the "Job Analysis of the Psychologist." The supervisor also makes available for study the case records, annual reports, and selected references on reading disability and psychodynamics.

3. *Supervision*

3.1 Of the Senior Psychologist

3.1.1 Following the orientation period, the senior psychologist should be able to work independently as a member of a clinic team. However, there should be regular consultation with the supervisor, usually on a monthly basis.

3.2 Of the Psychologist during the First Year of Service

3.2.1 The supervisor has responsibility, in consultation with the Director, for evaluating the work of the psychologist throughout this first year period. Consultations at least on a bi-weekly basis are advisable. The policy is to encourage the psychologist to present problems and to ask guidance in areas where he experiences a need and then to assist in every possible way. The supervisor is also expected to examine psychologist's records, read reports, and obtain information through direct observation.

3.2.2 The supervisor should write an evaluation of the new psychologist's work at the end of the year.

4. *Recruitment of Psychologists*

It is necessary for the supervisor, along with the Director, to engage in recruitment, to seek out and encourage qualified psychologists who may become interested in working in the reading clinics. Such persons are given appointments to visit the clinic and are interviewed by the Director and the Supervising Psychologist.

5. *Evaluation and Research*

5.1 The Supervising Psychologist should assist the Director in completing annual statistical reports concerned with the evaluation of the work of the reading clinic.

5.2 An evaluation of senior psychologists should be drawn up cooperatively.

5.3 It should also be the responsibility of the supervisor of psychologists to assist those who are studying toward the Ph.D. degree in planning research projects which are of theoretical or practical interest for the work with pupils having reading disability.

5.4 When, at the request of psychology staff members of the various colleges, graduate students ask cooperation from the reading clinic in psychological studies on various phases of reading disability, the Supervising Psychologist evaluates these requests; if it seems in the interest of the program of the reading clinic and the Director approves, the student is given appropriate assistance.

4.3.8 PROCEDURES

The Intake Study

After pupils have been referred to the reading clinic and have been tested and evaluated by the reading teacher, the clinical intake process is begun. The clinicians study the records. The social worker's first purpose is to determine for every case whether other community agencies are actively involved. If this is so, consultation with the other agency is necessary in order to determine whether it is appropriate for the reading clinic to accept the pupil. The psychologist examines the school records of the pupil in order to note if there are indications that he may suffer from general mental retardation rather than reading disability. In questionable cases, an individual examination to determine more exactly the pupil's mental ability is given as a first step in the intake process. It can then be established, by comparison of his actual reading achievement with his potential learning capacity, whether the boy or girl is a retarded reader in the sense that he is working below his intellectual capacity, and meets this criterion for selection.

In the usual referral to the clinic staff, the social worker begins work on a case by interviewing the parent—most often the mother, but sometimes the father and, in the absence of parents, the child's guardian. The social worker's interview is focused around the parent's recognition of the child's reading retardation and her attitude towards the child and his difficulties. At the same time, the social worker is evaluating the parent's capacity and accessibility for continued involvement in behalf of her child.

Other aspects of the first contacts of the social worker with the parent are the orientation of the mother to the program and to the services it makes available to her, recognizing the positive elements in the parent-child relationship, giving support to the mother in her role, and providing guidance in her handling of the child, which she can put to use immediately. At this time the parent is asked to sign a form indicating her consent to have the child in the reading program, and agreeing to cooperate with the social worker in keeping future appointments. The parent's agreement to have a psychiatric study of the child, if needed, is also included in this form.

PARENTAL CONSENT

Your child is being considered for special reading instruction. Each child who is accepted for this service will be given special reading instruction in a small group with a selected teacher, usually for two periods a week.

The school doctors have agreed to provide a physical check-up and an eye examination for every child in this program.

Please sign below to indicate your willingness to cooperate in this program, and to give consent for a medical examination and a psychiatric interview, if needed.

Yours truly,

———————————————————
Director

I hereby give permission for my (son, daughter)_____
to be given a medical examination and a psychiatric interview when necessary. I will also be available for appointments with the social worker.

———————————————   ———————————————
(date)   (signed)

The psychologist interviews the pupil in order to explore his interests, attitudes, and approaches to new situations. In this initial contact, a series of tests is given to obtain a psychological picture of the pupil. By this study the psychologist evaluates significant factors related to present intellectual functioning, possible neurological or organic impairment, personality structure, and possible areas of conflict in the pupil's emotional life.

The psychologist's initial interview with the boy or girl has a real impact. It provides for his orientation to the clinical program, and is his first acquaintance with the highly personalized nature of the clinical services. The pupil is told what the program is about, and what his part will be in it. He is helped to face his reading retardation and at the same time offered reassurance as to his ability and the staff members' conviction that he can achieve. He is encouraged to talk not only about his school life but also about his friends and his activities away from school. His competence in any area is thus brought out by the psychologist and experienced by the pupil as ego-nurturing. When a positive relationship is thereby established, the boy or girl is likely to accept readily any future contact for diagnosis or treatment.

The social worker and psychologist then review their findings together to determine whether further clinical study is necessary. A very small minority of pupils are refused because another type of service is more urgently needed before reading help can be offered. In such cases the social worker consults the parent, in order to facilitate referral of the boy or girl to the appropriate agency. The social worker discusses such a referral with the school principal. In all cases conferences are held with the reading clinic teacher and the clinic team to discuss the cases.

The Ongoing Clinical Program

In view of the fact that these boys and girls have both a reading disability and serious behavioral disturbances, it is not to be expected that all will be "smooth sailing" as soon as a pupil is accepted into the reading clinic. Though each pupil is an individual, different from all others, these pupils have usually lacked the recognition and approval that make the individual thrive. Even though the boy or girl is young and capable of change, certain unfavorable environmental influences, as well as negative self-attitudes, have already had damaging effect. The common goal of the social worker and psychologist, in cooperation with the reading clinic teacher, is to bring about changes in the pupil's life at school, at home, and in the community which will help him to become a happier and more successful individual. This requires thinking and working together and is described in an earlier section on "Clinic Day and the Team Approach." The psychologist and social worker are benefited by being able to read the anecdotal record in which the reading clinic teacher notes the pupil's responses to instruction and other significant behavior. Often the dynamics underlying his difficulties can be clarified by means of a conference scheduled for "clinic day." Sometimes symptomatic behavior which is a danger signal of serious maladjustment is thus revealed. As a result, further intensive work with the parent by the social worker must be arranged, and the psychologist may need to make a more detailed examination.

It is important for the staff of the reading clinic to communicate frequently with the class teacher, not less than twice a month. Although the reading clinic teacher is the one who usually maintains continuing contacts with the class teacher, if a pupil is showing behavior disorders of a serious nature, the reading teacher will usually call upon the clinical staff for help. In such situations a conference is usually arranged of all concerned with the individual pupil, including the class teacher and sometimes a supervisor. Here an attempt is made by the clinicians to bring out the causative factors, to clarify approaches which are indicated for the pupil's improvement, and to sustain the teacher in any positive and valuable handling which she may suggest. Sometimes it becomes necessary to ask that in order not to confuse the parent, the social worker rather than the class teachers handle serious problems with the parent.

In conferences with school supervisors the clinic team can sometimes be helpful in planning pupil's class placement with teachers who can best meet their needs. Such consultations are frequently requested by school supervisors.

Full Studies

A "full study" involves a psychiatric diagnosis, following the psychiatrist's interviews with both parent and child, and an evaluation by the clinical team of social worker, psychologist, and psychiatrist. Full studies are undertaken only in the most difficult cases—usually those which have not responded to the kinds of help generally offered to the disabled reader in the program.

After completion of the study, the data obtained are pooled in an "initial conference" in which the members of the three disciplines contribute their findings. The psychiatrist's contribution is often crucial in evaluating the severity of the emotional disturbance, the significance of neurological and medical findings, and the prognosis.

As a result of the "full study," specific recommendations are made for further treatment by reading clinic staff or referral to other sources of help. The social worker then arranges an interview with the parent in order to share the clinic staff members' impression of the pupil's needs and the recommendations which are to be considered. The parent becomes an active participant in working out whatever plan has been recommended and is given whatever help she needs in order to bring this about.

Treatment Services

In the broadest sense, the treatment functions performed by the clinical personnel are varied in nature. Even the first meeting with a parent and child may be therapeutic. It can make for some changes in their attitudes and inter-relationship which may improve the pupil's school adjustment, instructional or personal. The parent receives help from the social worker in facing the reading failure and her own feelings about it. The social worker's exploration of the background of the pupil's difficulties is professional and objective. An atmosphere in which acceptance of what is reported—without placing blame, and with a feeling of confidence that the situation can be helped—is maintained with the parent. Similarly, the pupil's difficulties are broached with him by the psychologist in an attitude of cooperative investigation. The psychologist attempts to convey a feeling of interest in and concern for the boy or girl, as well as respect for and confidence in his ability to overcome his difficulties. Thus, inherent in the intake study are the beginnings of a treatment process.

As more is learned about the maladjusted pupil, how he uses the reading room and how he relates to the reading clinic teacher, the clinic team may reconsider the initial findings to see how they apply to the pupil's behavior and the learning difficulty. The close contact which the clinic team has with the reading clinic teacher makes it possible to share thinking about the pupil's week-to-week progress, to evaluate readiness for revised plans, to test out and modify approaches to the pupil and his disability. An awareness of psychological forces that help determine a pupil's reading problem works toward helping the reading teacher provide a therapeutic climate in the reading room.

With more intensive clinical study of a pupil's inner life, and of the elements of the family constellation which affect his responses to school requirements, the clinic team can be helpful not only to the reading clinic teacher but also to the various school staff members who are important in the daily life of the boy or girl. Contacts planned and sustained over a critical period with the principal, guidance worker, or classroom teacher may help them to bring more understanding to their relationship with the pupil. Moreover, they thereby become more ready to carry forward certain cooperative measures affecting the pupil's school environment, such as class assignment and special handling when needed.

In selected cases, regular and continued contact with the parent and child, that is, treatment in the more usual sense, is provided by the clinic team. If the parents' difficulties in relation to the child are marked and the child is relatively free of internalized problems, only the parent is seen in regular treatment interviews by the social worker. In other cases, treatment is undertaken with the child only after a period of therapeutic exploration with the parent. This groundwork with the parent provides for a more responsive, flexible setting for the child to use—in defining his self-image, in acting out old and new ways of integrating feelings, and of using primary relationships more effectively for his growth.

Treatment of the pupil is provided usually by the psychologist or the psychiatrist in cases where the social worker is also treating the parents. This may be by means of an individual or a group process. Various kinds of groups are utilized according to the needs of the pupils and the aptitude of the therapist. Psychiatric consultation on treatment cases is an important part of the treatment process. On occasion, an outside consultant may be called in to help in the diagnosis and/or treatment.

Cooperation with Other Agencies

Some cases may be carried on a cooperative basis with other agencies. Referrals may come from varied and different social service agencies. In all instances, the pupil should be attending a school and should meet the criteria for referral to the reading clinic. When another agency is already active in working with him and his family, the agency social worker follows the same procedure as do classroom teachers in making referrals to the principal. Thus, the referral comes from the school principal, with the notation that the family and/or child is known to a certain community agency. The reading clinic social worker then arranges a conference with the agency social worker to discuss the case.

Though the reading clinic clinicians in general follow the usual procedures in the intake study of these cases, unnecessary duplication of work is avoided. For example, if a recent psychological and/or psychiatric examination of a pupil has been obtained by the other agency, these results should be made available to the reading clinic staff and should be included in the evaluation of the pupil's needs for instruction and handling. The social worker explains the cooperative aspect of the case to the parents and to school personnel. The community agency continues to have primary responsibility for treatment while the reading clinic social worker functions as a liaison between the community agency, the reading clinic teacher, and school personnel. The instructional program is provided by the reading clinic teacher.

There are times when the reading clinic social worker wishes to refer a case to a community agency for treatment while the child receives reading instruction in the reading clinic. Where such an arrangement is made, the reading clinic social worker becomes an important resource and consultative person to the agency worker. In instances of excessive absences from school by a pupil known to a reading clinic, every effort should be made to work cooperatively with the Attendance Officer. Classroom teachers are encouraged to follow already established procedure for reporting such absences.

In depressed areas the families of many pupils known to the reading clinic are recipients of public assistance. For most families, managing on a public assistance allowance is extremely difficult, and parents have been found to need help in budgeting, in anticipating the needs of their children and in planning accordingly. Welfare agencies should utilize the assistance of the reading clinic social worker in helping their clients to make the best possible use of their limited funds. For example, the welfare agency may give the reading clinic social worker a copy of the family's budget record, and in cases of special need, provide for the issuance of additional funds beyond the regular allowance issued for school-age children. It has been found that a cooperative relationship with the welfare agency investigator prevents many school absences due to inadequate clothing and other physical needs.

Follow-up and Articulation

There should be different kinds of follow-up of pupils who have been in the reading clinic program. The reading teacher's work with the alumni group, made up of those boys and girls who have reached grade level or better in reading, has been described earlier in this chapter in the section, " 'Graduation' and the 'Alumni Association.' " This alumni group should be tested each year to determine achievement in reading. Sometimes, because of continued emotional problems, some of these pupils should be retained in the regular caseload of a clinician to give support or other treatment as needed.

Of particular concern to the clinical staff every spring should be that group of older pupils who are to go on to a higher school the following term. Conferences should be held with the guidance counselor of the higher school in order to plan for the student's best placement in the new school. At this time, some of the pupil's problems, his reading growth and other evidences of progress, his ability as observed by individual examination and his needs should be discussed. These conferences of the reading clinic staff— clinicians and reading clinic teacher—with the higher school guidance counselor can be mutually helpful.

When a child and parent are under treatment or receiving counseling services, and it is felt inadvisable to terminate this service at the time when the pupil goes to a higher school, the clinician may continue the treatment of the parent or child. Students may return voluntarily to the clinic in order to discuss a problem which has arisen or to report on some achievement or experience of special interest. Many parents keep in touch with the social worker even though the pupil is no longer in the program.

4.3.9 STATISTICAL SUMMARIES OF THE WORK DONE BY THE CLINICIANS

At a date near the close of the school year, designated for the entire staff by the Director, annual statistics are closed so that summaries may be prepared for the annual report. The figures for each social worker, psychologist, and psychiatrist are available from the report forms which summarize case contacts and carry forward an up-to-date statistical summary.

The social worker's report shows the number of parents interviewed at intake and in treatment or counseling sessions. It also indicates the number of rejected, broken and cancelled appointments. Conferences of various types, involving the social worker with other staff members and school personnel, are listed separately. Workshops with parents and agency contacts are also recorded. (See "Social Worker's Numerical Summary of Case Contacts" on p. 68.)

Where there is more than one social worker, the data available on each worker's end-term summary are compiled and totaled by the Supervising Social Worker.

The annual summary of the psychologist's work is in three major categories (see "Psychologist's Numerical Summary of Case Contacts" on p. 73):

1. Number of contacts with or about pupils.
2. Number of pupils who have been given various types of psychological service.
3. Number of groups of pupils for whom psychologists have provided treatment.

Under (1.1), "Diagnostic contacts with pupils," there are included both the psychological intake studies and also the more intensive evaluations usually made at a later time. "Continuous contact interviews with pupils" (1.2) are those for counseling or treatment. "Parental interviews" by psychologists (1.3) are usually carried out in the presence of the social worker and always with the social worker's approval. The number of conferences about pupils are subdivided into (1.4) those "with other reading clinic staff members" and (1.5) those "with other school personnel." Provision is also made for recording the group tests administered (1.6) and for the use of other procedures (1.7).

Under section (2) the total number of individual pupils seen by psychologists is indicated, including numbers given (2.1) individual diagnostic study, (2.2) individual treatment, (2.3) individual counseling, and (2.4) group psychotherapy. Under (3) the total number of groups is recorded.

Where there is more than one clinic, the Supervising Psychologist prepares a numerical summary of the psychological work done in all of the clinic centers from the totals given on each psychologist's final weekly sheet. This summary, together with that prepared by the Supervising Social Worker, is presented to the Director of the reading clinics at the conclusion of each school year. Throughout the school year, the weekly report of the social worker and psychologist are given to the Director.

The annual summary of the psychiatrist's work should show the number of interviews with the child and the family; the total number of treatment cases seen, both child and parent; and the number of groups seen in therapy. There should be a summary of the conferences held with school personnel and agency personnel. The number of broken appointments should be indicated.

4.3.10 ANNUAL REPORTS OF CLINICAL STAFF

Each clinician, before the close of the school term, prepares an annual report in which he describes his assignment, gives an account of the major areas of his work, records the special problems he encountered, and tells about some of the aspects of the clinical work which he has found to be especially interesting and valuable. He may also make recommendations for changes in emphasis of the various aspects of his work. Usually, he describes the ways in which he feels that he has experienced professional growth and his plans for the future. References may be made to the progress of certain cases given counseling or intensive treatment.

4.3.11   RECORD KEEPING BY THE CLINICAL STAFF

The Pupil Folder—Clinical

The pupil folder should be set up by the social worker as soon as the selection data sheet has been completed by the reading clinic teacher. The child's name should be placed on the tab of the folder, last name first. The face sheet should be completed and should remain as the first page of the record. The selection data sheet should be kept in the folder until completion of the initial screening process and a disposition has been made. When the disposition has been entered on the selection sheet, it should then be returned to the reading clinic teacher to be filed in the pupil's instructional folder.

Forms which must be signed or completed during the initial interview should also be placed in the case record.

The social worker and psychologist should share responsibility for the keeping of the case record. The form, "Face Sheet," appears on page 92.

Recording the Initial Interview. The initial interview is the beginning of the social history. The social worker's name should be placed under the title. Identifying information, such as the pupil's name, parent's name, pupil's birth date, address, school, and grade should be placed in the upper right corner of the page. The page is numbered (1).

The first paragraph of the social history summarizes all pertinent information from the selection data sheet, along with any other available data, or observations made of the child and his situation. The content of the initial interview should follow.

Clearing with the Social Service Exchange (where such clearing agency exists). Where indicated, cases should be cleared with the Social Service Exchange. A request should be made for "information only" if there is some question regarding the eligibility of the pupil.

The Arrangement of the Clinical Materials. The recorded work of each discipline should be filed in the clinical folder in the following order:

The social history
The psychological evaluation, usually called "psychologist's notes"
The psychiatric evaluation or consultation

FACE SHEET

School_____   Date Accepted_____

Social Worker_____

Pupil's Name_____Sex____School_____Grade_____

_____   _____

_____   _____

Address_____Telephone_____

_____   _____

_____   _____

Birthplace_____Date of Birth_____

Parents: Father_____Address_____

     Mother_____Address_____
         Maiden Name—First Name

Brothers and Sisters:

Name	Age	School and Grade or Occupation
_____	_____	_____
_____	_____	_____
_____	_____	_____
_____	_____	_____
_____	_____	_____
_____	_____	_____

Reading Grades: Emergency address and telephone:

  Initial_____Employer of Mother_____

  Final_____   of Father_____

            Other Relative or Neighbor

The report of the initial conference

The reports of case conferences, the "Record of Case Conference" form.

The social worker's and psychologist's treatment notes should follow the initial conference. The work of each discipline should be clipped together.

Copies of letters, reports, etc., should be kept together in sequence, with the most recent date prominent.

Carbon copies of clinical material should follow the same order as above, and are kept in the back of the folder.

Psychological test booklets, drawings, scoring sheets, etc., dated and clipped together, should comprise the final section of the record.

Recording by the Social Worker. The social worker's recording should be as clear and concise as possible. The first few interviews should be descriptive of how the client reacts to the interview and includes the interaction between the client and the social worker. It should record how the client sees his problems and the social worker's evaluation of the client's accessibility for further exploration and treatment.

Treatment interviews should be summarized at regular intervals. In this kind of recording the social worker should keep notes of the significant aspects of each interview, and where necessary, be specific about particular incidents, dates, names, changes in attitudes, or changes in the treatment relationship.

Clinic conferences, whether initial, consultation or treatment, should be summarized by the social worker and filed in the appropriate place in the case record.

The case conference should be reported jointly by the reading clinic teacher, psychologist and social worker, in duplicate. Copies should be filed in the clinical and instructional records.

Recording by the Psychologist. The psychologist is responsible for recording the results of each examination of a pupil. The form and content vary with the occasion (whether an "intake" study or an examination for a more complete diagnosis) and with the nature of the pupil's problems. Though there is no set outline to be followed, each report should include the exact name of the child, his date of birth, school, grade, date of examination, the name of the psychologist, a statement of the pupil's referral problems, a listing of the psychological techniques used and a summary of findings.

These reports, when typed, should be checked and signed by the psychologist before being filed in the case record.

Recording by the Psychiatrist. The psychiatrist should dictate diagnostic evaluations and treatment notes following each session with a pupil. These are signed and placed in the clinical case record.

Auxiliary Services. *The physical examination.* The medical history form is usually filled out following the initial interview. The form should be made out in duplicate and both copies forwarded to the school nurse. When the forms have been completed by the pediatrician at the time of the physical examination, the original should be returned to the social worker to be filed in the clinical record. The ophthalmological and/or optometric examination should be recorded. (The speech diagnosis is contained in the instructional folder.)

Case Closing. When a case is closed, the recording should be brought up to date. The last sentence of the summary states the reason and gives the date of closing. The reason for closing (graduated, transferred, or moved out of the district) should be recorded on the outside of the folder.

The records of closed cases should be transferred to the closed file.

Notations on the Caseload Sheet

The clinicians should make entries on the caseload sheets each month as follows:

The Social Worker's Notations. Services given to parents are indicated with an entry of "I" for interview, "C" for consultation, and "T" for treatment. When pediatric and ophthalmological and/or optometric examinations are completed, appropriate columns are checked. Service by the psychiatrist is indicated with "D" for diagnosis and "T" for treatment.

The Psychologist's Notations. Entries of "D" and "T" are made as psychological study and/or treatment are provided. The psychologist also records IQ's obtained on Stanford-Binet or WISC examinations in spaces provided.

Work Schedules and Cumulative Statistics

The social worker and the psychologist should keep daily schedules of appointments kept, cancelled, or broken. Each Friday a revised copy of the past week's schedule should be completed and submitted, along with the advanced schedule for the next week, to the Director.

Weekly statistical summary sheets of the various clinical services should be compiled by the social worker and psychologist and submitted on Monday of each week to the Director.

Psychologist's Statistical Record Form

This record card should be maintained by the psychologist for each pupil who is examined individually. Spaces are provided for entering essential identifying information, the numerical results of certain intelligence and achievement tests and all dates when psychological techniques have been used with the child. The card lists the various projective tests and other procedures (including diagnostic and treatment interviews) so that dates and the examiner's name can be readily recorded in the appropriate spaces. Places are also given for entering dates of consultations regarding the pupil with other clinical or school staff members and of group conferences concerning the child.

On the following pages appears the form, "Psychologist's Statistical Record."

Staff Development Programs for the Clinicians

It is important to plan and organize some procedure for communication among staff members of the several professional disciplines. This needs to be done to provide for mutual stimulation and improvement of work. For this purpose regular monthly meetings of the reading clinic psychologists and social workers should be held as well as workshops and seminars.

Announcements of special programs and course offerings should be brought to the attention of the staff and the staff members should be encouraged to enroll. At future staff meetings discussion may center around these special programs. Invited speakers may be another source of inspiration. Opportunities to observe individual and group therapy sessions through one-way vision screens (if available) followed by discussion is another procedure for up-grading staff knowledge and skills.

Participation in conferences and convention programs affords an opportunity for the staff to experience further stimulation and improvement of the work. Additional sources of training should be brought about through meetings and conferences with community agencies. Such meetings should be carefully structured so that an exchange and a sharing of experiences can be mutually enriching.

PSYCHOLOGIST'S STATISTICAL RECORD

Name_____ Boy___Girl___Date of Birth_____ Sch._____ Cl._____

Reading Readiness (date and score) _____

Group Tests (date and score) _____

	Date	Examiner	CA	MA	IQ	Further Evaluation	Date	Examiner	Notes
S. Binet Form						Bender Gestalt			
WISC Verbal						Blacky Test			
WISC Performance						CAT			
WISC Full Scale						Color Vision			
						Diag. Interview			
						Harris Laterality			
						Hum. Fig. Draw.			
						Other Drawings			
Initial Study					Notes	Keystone VS & P			
Rosenzweig P.F.						Rorschach			
Diagnostic Interview						Rosenzweig			
Human Fig. Draw.						TAT			
Bender Gestalt						Tendler Compl.			
						Other			

IQ

Name of Test

[The reverse side of this form appears on the next page.]

Treatment Interviews of Pupil by Psychologist: _____

   Dates: _____ _____ _____ _____ _____ _____

              _____ _____ _____ _____ _____ _____

              _____ _____ _____ _____ _____ _____

              _____ _____ _____ _____ _____ _____

              _____ _____ _____ _____ _____ _____

Group Therapy with Psychologist: _____

   Dates: _____ _____ _____ _____ _____ _____

              _____ _____ _____ _____ _____ _____

              _____ _____ _____ _____ _____ _____

              _____ _____ _____ _____ _____ _____

              _____ _____ _____ _____ _____ _____

Consultations of Psychologist: _____

   With Social Worker _____ _____ _____ _____

       Psychiatrist _____ _____ _____ _____

       Reading Clinic Teacher _____ _____ _____ _____

        _____ _____ _____ _____ _____

       Supervisor _____ _____ _____ _____

       Class Teacher (Name) _____ _____ _____ _____

       Others _____ _____ _____ _____

Group Conferences re Pupil (Enter dates)

   With S.W. and R.C.T. _____ _____ _____ _____

        _____ _____ _____ _____

   With Clinic Team _____ _____ _____ _____

        _____ _____ _____ _____

Staff-School Conf.

Date	Present
_____	_____
_____	_____

Reading

	Date	Test	Form	Grade Score	Notes
on adm. RC	_____	_____	_____	_____	_____
	_____	_____	_____	_____	_____
Final Score	_____	_____	_____	_____	_____

5 THE REMEDIAL READING TEACHER

5.1 WHO SHALL BE A REMEDIAL READING TEACHER?

The position of the remedial reading teacher has existed in some communities over the past decades. In more recent years this position has been established in a rapidly increasing number of communities for the purpose of improving the reading level of pupils who have not successfully learned to read in the regular classroom. This position frequently has different titles and in some school systems may be known as reading specialist, special reading teacher, or corrective reading teacher.

The remedial reading teacher's primary function is to service retarded readers in the elementary or junior or senior high schools. A secondary function is to assist the supervisors in upgrading instruction in reading. The qualifications for the selection of the remedial reading teacher may vary from community to community; in some states, certification requirements have been drawn up for the position; in other school systems, the remedial reading teacher is selected by supervisors. Experience in teaching in an elementary or secondary school for not less than three years should be a basic requirement for the remedial reading teacher; specialized preparation through graduate courses in the teaching of reading, including a practicum, should also be a requisite.

More important than the knowledges and skills and academic background of the remedial reading teacher is the kind of person she is and how she feels about working with children who have not been successful learners. Of course, the goal is to improve poor reading. But what takes place between the teacher and learner must come first; reading improvement will follow. The remedial reading teacher must respect this pupil; must diagnose and look for causes in order to help him overcome difficulties; must recognize his strengths; must convey to him through the interactions that take place her belief in his ultimate success. Poor reading has many symptoms and the sensitive, perceptive, skillful teacher recognizes them and deals with them.

5.2 GOALS AND OBJECTIVES

For the pupil: To improve his attitude toward reading, to raise his level of achievement in reading and, generally, to bring about a more favorable personal-social development.

For the classroom teacher: To help the teacher to recognize the nature of the problems of the individual child with reading disability and to help plan a program for improving and/or correcting the diagnosed needs.

For the parent: To guide parents to understand their child's reading problem and to involve them in a cooperative plan to help their child.

For the school, the community: To share with the school and the community knowledges and techniques through reports, conferences, and seminars.

5.3 SELECTION OF PUPILS

Pupils should be referred by the principal, homeroom teacher, or the chairman of the English department. The class teacher or homeroom or English teacher will make the recommendation based on the criteria which appear here. The number of students referred should have a relationship to the number of vacancies. If the remedial reading teacher is in an elementary school, it is advisable that the boys and girls selected for special help should be of the second, third and fourth grades. In upper schools, the students referred for special help should be selected as early after admission as possible.

With the foregoing as an important consideration, the following criteria for selection apply:

For the elementary schools: (1) Reading retardation of two years if the pupil is in fourth grade and correspondingly greater or less retardation if the child is in a higher or lower grade than fourth; (2) Evidence that the pupil has at least "average" mental ability.

For the higher schools: (1) Reading retardation of two or more years for grade; (2) Evidence that the student has at least "average" mental ability.

In selecting students in elementary or high schools, it is important to note that an evaluation of reading retardation based on standardized silent reading tests can only be an approximation. These grade scores involve a certain chance of error and guessing. The essential factors that should be taken into consideration are a comparison of the pupil's reading achievement with the pupil's expected achievement for his grade placement, his chronological age, his school history and his estimated mental maturity.

In regard to "average" mental ability (both in elementary and higher schools) the purpose is to select pupils whose achievement is below that which is expected of pupils of his mental maturity. The reason for this criterion is to exclude the mentally retarded pupil who is actually not retarded in reading, perhaps, but is manifesting one aspect of a slower developmental process. Such pupils need a modified curriculum. Nevertheless, caution is necessary to insure that the pupils who are retarded in reading are not regarded as mentally retarded. The class or homeroom or English teacher can observe the pupil and may get additional assistance by using the outline prepared for this purpose. (On p. 24 appears "A Guide to Teachers' Estimates of Intelligence of Pupils Retarded in Reading.")

5.4   DIAGNOSIS

After a pupil is referred to her, the remedial reading teacher examines the record card, health card, and any other pertinent data, such as guidance material, test data, etc. She should confer with the class teacher in elementary school or subject teachers (English, social studies, science, etc.) in the higher schools to gather further information about the pupil. This data should be recorded on a "Selection Data" form which appears on p. 25. At this point, the remedial reading teacher should administer an appropriate standardized achievement test. During this testing session she should make observations and note them down. These observations may help her in understanding the pupil's needs and developing more effective procedures in planning the instructional program. The tests are scored and checked a second time. It is suggested that she determine the "reading accuracy." A pupil's "reading accuracy rating" is based on the number of correct items divided by the number of attempted items. In interim or end-term evaluations, another means of measuring a pupil's reading improvement is provided by a comparison of the initial accuracy rating and subsequent ones.

A more technical reading diagnosis is necessary. It is necessary to know the specific weaknesses and defects and also to learn which skills have been mastered. This diagnosis should be informal and formal. An informal reading inventory should be administered. The form "An Analysis of Reading Difficulties" which appears on p. 51 may be used as a check-list and analyzed as part of this reading inventory; it may also serve to give the remedial reading teacher an appraisal of the student's functional level of reading. More formal tests that can be used are the Gilmore Oral Reading Test and the Gray Standardized Oral Reading Check-Tests. Graded word lists should also be employed to determine the level at which a pupil can recognize words at sight; and this provides information regarding the pupil's competence in word-attack skills.

Before the instructional program gets into its initial stages, the remedial reading teacher should confer with the school nurse and the class teacher. Any physical defects that she may be observing should be brought to their attention and plans for corrective measures initiated. The remedial reading teacher must constantly be on the alert to note the pupil's vision and hearing. How does he hold his book? Is his face furrowed as he reads? Does he squint? Does he seem uncomfortable? Does he favor one ear over the other? Is he overweight? Underweight? Is he unduly restless? These are but a few of the physical factors that the remedial reading teacher should be watching for and, where necessary, should confer about with school health personnel, classroom teacher, supervisor, and parent.

5.5 GROUPING FOR INSTRUCTION

In analyzing the boys and girls to determine which groups to assign them to and how to schedule them, it would seem a simple matter to set up certain objective criteria and then proceed. The objective criteria for determining group placement would be similar reading difficulties, similar reading needs, the same age and the same grade. However, the schedules of the school, the class program, and the pupils' interest and enthusiasm for certain subjects, such as, health education, shop, or enthusiasm for a special teacher, need to be considered if the pupil is to come to this reading instruction with a sense of excitement, an eagerness, a high level of interest, and an active willingness to participate. No doubt when a reading group is comprised of students from different classes and sometimes different grades the scheduling is complicated. It is advisable to cooperate with the class teacher, or the homeroom teacher, and the English teacher. In this way the best interests of the pupils will be served. The most important factor that should be observed in grouping pupils is to assign those boys and girls to learn together who can be expected to work together with success both in reading attainment and in personality relationships. Sex of the pupil may sometimes be an important consideration when grouping students in the middle grades and higher. It is important that the remedial reading teacher tell the pupils that these groups are not permanent and that it may be necessary to make changes from time to time.

Since diagnosis is continuous, the remedial reading teacher will note, as she works with each group, the differences among students in their acquisition of new knowledges and skills; in their ability to work independently; in their attitudes toward this new learning experience; in their ability to assume responsibilities. The remedial reading teacher must be ever aware of the levels of development of these pupils and as soon as any students have moved beyond the group, they must be changed to another group where they can be stimulated and encouraged to work towards new goals.

5.6   PLANNING FOR INSTRUCTION

Plans need to be developed for each group based on the diagnosed reading needs. The retarded reader is usually very constricted in his thinking, very self-involved, and cannot create situations nor raise questions nor attempt discussions. The remedial reading teacher needs to plan in such detail so that the pupils' efforts are carefully directed.

The remedial reading teacher must gather all her creative skill in developing highly motivated situations that will stimulate the students. Teacher-prepared materials are a resource for pupil stimulation oftentimes. Pupils' interests need to be explored and reading materials provided that will be related to these interests. A form called "Lesson Plan" appears on p. 43.

Another essential aspect of the work of the remedial reading teacher is that she needs to be continuously aware of each pupil's needs while maintaining a unity of structure in the work with the group. This helps the students to develop a sense of identity with the group. This group identification contributes greatly towards increased learning. There is a commonality of need and in this is found a resource of strength and a new confidence to move forward.

The Instructional Hour

Often, the question is asked as to how the instructional hour is to be planned so that the maximum use of this time can be achieved. It is the authors' experience in observing different remedial reading teachers at work over a period of years that the optimal use of this instructional hour is to provide: group motivation, skill development for all the students, group discussion or learning experience or question period, carefully planned independent reading followed by independent seat-work activities or exercises. During this independent seat-work, the remedial reading teacher works with the pupils individually. This is concluded with a brief group discussion and review of the session. For the young pupil, the session should provide short, varied activities in order to maintain a high level of sustained interest.

5.7   MATERIALS OF INSTRUCTION

The instructional materials should include teacher-prepared materials, experience charts, original devices, varied levels of trade books and workbooks in different curriculum areas, such as literature, social studies, science, home economics and mathematics.

Magazines for the young pupil as well as those of interest to the student in the higher schools should be available. There should be sufficient books to enable the pupils to borrow for home reading. If the supply of books in a particular area is limited and the students have expressed an interest in this subject, the remedial reading teacher should bring in additional material from her local library or other sources which she may have access to.

The many commercial reading games—and some that the remedial reading teacher may develop—can be a motivating force in engaging the pupils' interest. The remedial reading teacher should develop numerous devices that will serve to reinforce reading skills; some of these devices can be developed with the students. Pictures, brief newspaper clippings, cartoons can be another resource. There are also the many workbooks and skill development materials produced commercially which can be of value. In appendix C appears a listing of books, used by remedial reading and reading clinic teachers, which have been found worthwhile.

5.8   THE WEEKLY SCHEDULE, THE DAILY SCHEDULE, AND THE CASELOAD OF THE REMEDIAL READING TEACHER

The question of how often pupils should be seen for instruction is asked very frequently—that is, how may sessions a week. There has been little research on this subject. Precedent favored daily sessions. One of the authors on the basis of previous experience and for the best deployment of staff believed that two reading periods a week were adequate. In her work this plan was put into effect. Several years later a study on optimum number of reading sessions per week was conducted and is reviewed on p. 29.

A typical schedule of a remedial reading teacher should include instruction for four groups of pupils on Monday and Thursday and four different groups on Tuesday and Friday. Each session should be about fifty minutes. A group should generally consist of a maximum of eight students. The program should be set up so the pupils are seen at the same hour on each of the two days. The fifth hour of each day is used to see some students alone, either because they have been absent or there is a need for this additional individual instruction. This hour may also be used to develop further reading diagnosis of some students, preparation of materials, and maintenance of the reading room. The reading room used by the remedial reading teacher should be attractively set up and replete with techniques and devices. It should be a resource room for teachers to visit. Wednesday, an unassigned teaching day, is the time set aside for conferring with the class teacher whose pupils are in the program; conferring with parents; demonstrations for teachers selected by the supervisor; meetings with groups of teachers selected by the principal for discussion on a specific area in reading; or a workshop on techniques and devices conducted in the remedial reading room and scheduled by the supervisor.

5.9 THE REMEDIAL READING TEACHER AND THE CLASSROOM TEACHER, SUPERVISORS AND OTHER PROFESSIONAL PERSONNEL

The remedial reading teacher's assignment has two aspects. The major one is to work with groups of retarded readers and the other is to serve as a resource person to the school personnel. In her role as a remedial reading teacher, the students are referred to her by the principal or supervisor or department chairman. Such referrals, as has been mentioned earlier, usually have been initiated by the class teacher, homeroom, or English teacher. In the selection process, the remedial reading teacher confers with the class teacher. After the pupil is taken into the program, the remedial reading teacher sets up a scheduled plan of meetings, twice a month, with the class, homeroom, or English teacher of the pupil in the remedial program. The purpose of such conferences is to involve this teacher as one of the team working with the student. There is an exchange of information, diagnostic findings are shared, special approaches and techniques are discussed. Very often some of the suggestions made by the remedial reading teacher are utilized by the class teacher with other students for whom she thinks this approach may be effective, too.

The remedial reading teacher may be called upon by the supervisor to participate in a faculty conference or a departmental meeting, lead a discussion with a group of newly appointed teachers, provide demonstration lessons, illustrate the use of teacher-prepared or commercial materials, have teachers visit the reading room to gather ideas for the development of new and different approaches and techniques. The remedial reading teacher may look to the supervisor for the budgetary allotment to provide the program with adequate materials of instruction. The supervisor should plan cooperatively with the remedial reading teacher the scheduling of reading conferences, workshops, demonstrations, etc. Any administrative problems should be brought to the attention of the supervisor.

The guidance staff, speech improvement teacher, school nurse and school doctor are important members of the program. The remedial reading teacher should seek their cooperation in situations that need their guidance and help.

5.10   THE REMEDIAL READING TEACHER AND THE PARENTS

To insure the most effective results in her work with the pupil, the remedial reading teacher involves the parent as early as possible. When the
pupil is accepted into the program, she meets with the parent. In this
initial conference, she explains the program and the role of the parent.
For some parents, it may be sufficient to know that a special service is
being provided and they can relax their pressures on the pupil. This may
be their most effective role. If they can accept this, the conference may
be concluded with the setting of a date for a second conference at a
future time.

There will be other parents who may need to be more actively involved.
These are the parents who should be given some simple games or devices
to work with their boy or girl. Careful guidance by the remedial reading
teacher in the use of this material is most important and should include a
discussion of the parent-child relationships during this tutoring session.
For other parents, it may be helpful to plan a few workshops to discuss
the instructional program in reading. As many parents as can be invited
should come to participate in this workshop. For all these parents, there
should be an opportunity to observe the remedial reading program at
least twice a year.

Above all, the remedial reading teacher should help all the parents to
see their most important role—that of "being a parent." Such a role
includes reading to the boy or girl, trips and family outings, visits to the
public library, providing for the boy or girl books, magazines and newspapers, and conveying to him or her through attitudes, feelings and actions
an understanding, a sensitivity, an awareness of needs and a respect for the
dignity of the individual.

5.11   RECORD KEEPING

The day a student is referred for remedial reading, data begins to be
accumulated. All of this should be organized and recorded so as to be
used efficiently. There needs to be a folder for each pupil, preferably

legal size, with the student's name and grade. The folder should have the following contents and should be kept in this order:

The Selection Data Sheet. This sheet contains identifying data, statements regarding reasons for referral, and other notations. (Referred to on p. 24. The form appears on p. 25.)

A Report from the Speech Improvement Teacher. Each pupil's speech should be evaluated by the speech teacher and a written report given to the remedial reading teacher. The statement is brief and indicates any defects and makes recommendation for treatment. The remedial reading teacher notes the time of the treatment program and avoids any conflict of scheduling.

An Analysis of Reading Difficulties. (The use of this form is described on p. 50.)

Reading Tests. The tests used for original measurement, the diagnostic tests, and those used for evaluation are retained in this pupil folder. Scores should be noted on a summary sheet stapled on the inside cover of the folder. (See p. 57 for the form, "Record of Reading Tests.") The remedial reading teacher should refer back to the student's work on a standardized test in order to check the specific nature of his difficulties.

Caseload Record. The remedial reading teacher should maintain an up-to-date list of the students in her caseload. This should contain: name, date of birth, intelligence test scores (if available), evidence of a speech diagnosis, any physical examinations that have been administered, the original achievement test score and subsequent tests, reading retardation in months and years, reading gains.

Record of In-Service Teacher Education. Reference has been made to the work with the class teachers, not only those whose pupils are in the program, but other teachers selected by the supervisor who will observe the program, visit the reading room, participate in an individual or group conference. (The form on which this aspect of the program is recorded appears on p. 63.)

Evaluation: (See Chapter 7 on Evaluation).

6 THE READING CONSULTANT

6.1 WHO SHALL BE A READING CONSULTANT?

The reading consultant should be an outstanding teacher who has demonstrated not only skill and competence in the teaching of reading but also creativity and curiosity in wanting to try new and different approaches. This position is a very sensitive one in that it involves working not only with children but also working closely with supervisors, classroom teachers and reading teachers. Her personality should serve to inspire and stimulate those with whom she comes in contact so that they can see the teaching of reading as an exciting adventure.

The reading consultant should have at least three years experience as a classroom teacher on varying grade and age levels. In addition to the usual courses in developmental reading, and diagnosis and correction of reading difficulties, the reading consultant should have a background of a practicum in reading, and organization and supervision of reading improvement programs. This background of knowledge is essential in setting up reading improvement programs for individual schools and groups of schools.

6.2   GOALS AND OBJECTIVES

For the classroom teacher: to help the teacher to diagnose pupils' needs and to plan a program for continuously upgrading the instruction in reading. This is the major function of the reading consultant.

For the pupil: through the cooperative efforts of the reading consultant and the classrom teacher the continuous upgrading of the instructional program should help to improve the attitude of the pupil toward reading and to raise the level of achievement.

For the parent: to guide parents to understand how pupils learn to read and to involve them in the program to help their child.

For the School: to plan with the supervisor reading improvement programs which will upgrade the instructional level of the school.

For the community: to share with the community knowledges and techniques through reports, conferences, workshops and seminars.

6.3   SELECTION OF SCHOOLS

In smaller communities the reading consultant may be scheduled by the superintendent to serve in all of the schools. In the larger communities the local superintendent should select the schools and schedule with the reading consultant the length of service for each of these schools. These schedules may vary with each of the school situations, taking into consideration size of staff, quality of instruction in reading, needs of pupils, readiness and availability of the teaching corps and supervisors for this service.

6.4   THE READING CONSULTANT
AND THE SUPERVISOR

In the elementary schools, the reading consultant should confer with the principal of the school to which she has been assigned to help set up a reading improvement program. This may mean setting up a program of in-service education for new staff members; planning a reading improvement program with emphasis on the prevention of reading retardation; setting up a special program for the disabled readers; demonstrating the administration and interpretation of standardized tests as well as the informal inventory; helping classroom teachers in the diagnosis of reading disabilities; planning a program of remediation; helping the staff in selecting appropriate materials of instruction; keeping the staff abreast of the most recent literature and research in the field.

In consultation with the principal, the reading consultant should set up short term workshops on special aspects of the teaching of reading requested by staff and/or supervisor. If there is a need for planning a program of remediation with disabled readers the reading consultant should organize and demonstrate the procedures for the selection of these pupils; the screening process; the diagnostic procedures to be followed; the grouping for instruction; the planning for instruction; the materials of instruction; evaluation procedures to be followed. (For the preceding, except evaluation, see chapter 5, "The Remedial Reading Teacher"; for evaluation, see chapter 7, "Evaluation of a Special Reading Program.")

In the higher schools, similar patterns of work may be followed. Here it will be necessary for the reading consultant to work with principals, heads of departments and classroom teachers. Procedures for setting up workshops, demonstrations and sessions for retarded readers will have to be scheduled in conjunction with the ongoing total school program. In the case of an entire class of retarded readers, the department chairman, the class teacher and the reading consultant should plan together a reading improvement program in the subject area concerned.

The teaching of reading in the content areas is a major concern in secondary schools. The reading consultant should work closely with the department heads in curriculum areas where reading retardation is interfering appreciably with the students' comprehension of the curriculum content. It may be necessary to arrange short workshops in reading conducted by the reading consultant in which selected topics are discussed, for example, How To Give an Informal Reading Inventory, Development of Vocabulary for Use in a Specific Content Area, How to Increase Comprehension Skills in a Specific Content Area, etc.

In those curriculum areas in the secondary school which are programmed daily, the reading consultant should discuss with the department head and the class teachers the advisability of using one session weekly for the teaching of reading. This procedure has been found useful, particularly when a carefully worked out reading improvement program has been followed. Where a remedial reading teacher is also available such sessions should form part of her assignment.

The head of the English department and the reading consultant should confer regarding the role of the English teachers in furthering reading improvement programs for the school. Should the English teachers be responsible for teaching of reading in content areas other than English? Should the English teachers become sufficiently expert in the teaching of reading so that they become resource personnel for teachers in the other content areas? The answers to these questions should be discussed by principal, department head, and reading consultant. The answers will vary with the composition of the staff and the needs of the particular school.

6.5 THE READING CONSULTANT AND THE CLASSROOM TEACHER

Working with classroom teachers to improve the teaching of reading is the primary function of the reading consultant. In the elementary school, the principal (or his assistant) may find it necessary to involve the reading consultant in the developmental program of the school as a whole. In other instances, the principal may request the reading consultant to develop reading improvement programs for new teachers. Again, the principal may ask the reading consultant to set up a program to improve the reading of disabled readers.

In setting up a program of remediation, there are administrative problems to be resolved by the principal. Class teachers have to be released to attend workshop sessions, to observe demonstrations given by the reading consultant, to work with small groups of disabled readers preferably from their own classes. Workshop sessions should deal with high priority topics; for example, the teaching of specific phonics and word analysis skills, the teaching of specific vocabulary or comprehension skills.

Demonstrations with classes or small groups of pupils should be given by the reading consultant. At the close of the demonstration there should be a follow-up discussion with the classroom teachers. This, in turn, should lead to observations by the reading consultant of follow-up lessons by the classroom teachers. An individual conference with each teacher should follow. This interaction of classroom teacher and reading consultant is inherent in a sound program for upgrading the instruction of reading.

A plan for improvement in the teaching of reading in upper grade schools involves other facets: administrative problems arising because of the departmentalized programs in these schools and the specialized training of the secondary school teacher. Scheduling of teachers and pupils to work with the reading consultant should be arranged by the various department heads. Details of the work of the reading consultant in a secondary school are discussed under the preceding section, "The Reading Consultant and the Supervisor."

6.6 THE READING CONSULTANT AND THE PUPIL

The reading consultant works with pupils usually in a demonstration setting. These demonstrations may include the techniques of the diagnostic procedures, informal and formal testing, techniques and procedures in the instructional program, providing for individual differences, evaluation procedures. In addition the reading consultant should assist in the selection of pupils for a program of remediation. The consultant should make referrals to a remedial reading teacher in a nearby school (if none is available in the school) or to a community agency that may service these pupils, or, if the pupil needs more intensive service, to a reading clinic.

6.7 THE READING CONSULTANT AND THE READING RESOURCE ROOM

Where space is available in assigned schools, the reading consultant should set up a reading resource room. This room should contain materials related to the workshop sessions, techniques, and devices that will help the teachers. The resource rooms in the assigned schools should not be uniform as they reflect differing needs in the various schools. Charts, ditto materials found useful in teaching particular skills, new books for pupils, recently published professional books and journals should be attractively displayed. The resource room should be readily available to the classroom teacher and should be utilized whenever possible for grade, group, or curriculum area conferences.

6.8   THE READING CONSULTANT AND EVALUATION

In the evaluation of the reading program of a school, the reading consultant can serve as a valuable resource person. The supervisor may use the reading consultant's services to help new and untrained teachers administer informal and standardized tests. For the retarded readers, the reading consultant should be called in to help in diagnosis—the first step in evaluation. Where many members of the staff require assistance in administration of a particular evaluative procedure, the principal or department head should request the reading consultant's help. A more extended description of the evaluation of a special reading program is given in the next chapter.

7 EVALUATION OF A SPECIAL READING PROGRAM

Before it is possible to speak in detail regarding procedures for evaluating special help programs in reading, it is important that the aims, scope, and design of the particular program be spelled out. Any program of special services in reading, be it a remedial reading or a reading clinic program, should have a comprehensive program of evaluation built into the overall structure.

If the special program for the retarded readers covers a geographic area which is clearly delimited, the superintendent of the district will require certain reports. He will expect to receive at the close of the school term (or at other specially requested periods) a report in general pupil-accounting terms. For example, the total number of pupils receiving service will be reported, and perhaps this figure will be set against the number of pupils referred for service and the number discharged, with reasons given. Some superintendents will want to evaluate how the various schools are taking advantage of such a special service and may want the data broken down by schools.

7.1 INITIAL STAGES IN EVALUATION

Pupils who suffer from reading disabilities are usually referred for service to a remedial reading teacher or a reading clinic by their class or English teacher, and/or the school principal, and/or other interested school personnel. Usually the pupil's parents are informed and should have some part in the plan. The first steps taken by the remedial reading teacher or the reading clinic teacher is a diagnosis of this pupil's reading pattern. The pupil will have several reading tests—to measure reading achievement and to analyze special difficulties in reading such as are revealed by various tests of phonic, word analysis and comprehension skills. Objective scores obtained on reading tests will have been recorded in terms of age or grade scores, percentile points, etc., which will serve as a basis for measuring later improvement.

The reading clinic teacher will also have learned from the regular school staff what behavior and/or personality problems the child manifests so that these reports, together with her own first observations of behavior, may be entered in the anecdotal record and later used as a basis for evaluation of changes in behavior. Many remedial reading teachers may also want to make note of the classroom teacher's remarks concerning this pupil's behavior for comparison at another time. Depending on the extent to which the parents are concerned with the pupil's difficulty and can contribute their own observations and expression of attitudes, the parent-child relationships can provide further information and should be assessed for their bearing upon the child's learning and behavior difficulties. Special cases may include those needing individual medical attention, eye or ear specialists, correction of sensory defects, or assistance with a related problem such as speech defects. Notations concerning all of these conditions must be entered in the case records so that their handling may not be overlooked nor their later evaluation omitted in regard to the response to such treatment.

Another more informal method which includes evaluation in a consultation procedure is followed in the programs in which the authors have been involved. On the one specified day per week when the remedial reading teacher is not scheduled to meet with the groups of pupils for remedial instruction, a part of this day should include scheduled conferences with the class or English teacher or other school personnel. During these conferences, there should be a periodic, interim evaluation of the pupils' reading progress. There should be an exchange of diagnosed needs and agreement as to the best procedures. These conferences should be recorded in the pupils' record.

For the reading clinic teacher on the one day per week when she is not scheduled for reading instruction with the boys and girls, conferences should be scheduled with the clinic staff—the psychologist and social worker and, in special cases, with the psychiatrist. These may be "intake" conferences—when the purpose is to share information and interpretations made from the initial studies. Plans as to the type of handling the pupil may need are agreed upon by the staff members and are recorded in a special report, copies of which are placed both in the pupil's instructional folder and in the clinical folder. This form has been mentioned earlier. It is known as the "Record of Case Conference" and appears on page 59. Later conferences may be held again—especially if the child does not respond to the reading instruction as had been anticipated. Very often such full team conferences should include the class or English teacher or other school personnel. The reading clinic teacher meets with the class teacher of the pupils she is servicing twice a month for conferences. These conferences include a discussion of diagnostic needs, of techniques most appropriate in the handling of this pupil, and an evaluation of the pupil's reading progress. All of these group processes, which certainly lead to closer cooperation of the various people concerned with the individual pupil (such as the remedial reading teacher, the class or English teacher, or other school personnel; or the reading clinic teacher, the class teacher, the psychologists and social workers) involve evaluation directly or indirectly.

7.2   INTERIM OR YEAR-END EVALUATION— THE TESTING PROGRAM

A more general evaluation of the reading progress made of pupils in the remedial reading program or in a reading clinic is the regular program for retesting the pupils with alternate equivalent forms of the same reading tests or with succeeding tests included in the same series given previously. Hopefully, scores on such tests are graded on the same scale or by age or grade standards which have known and equivalent units.

The obvious way to evaluate the reading achievement of a pupil or group of pupils is to compare the scores obtained in reading tests at the close of a school term or after a significant length of time during which special help was given, be it remedial reading or reading clinic, with the scores obtained at the beginning of such a period of special service. Reading gains are obtained by simple subtraction of the original from the subsequent or terminal grade scores.

7.3 YEAR-END EVALUATION— RATIO OF LEARNING

Another evaluative procedure which can be very significant is based on a pupil's ratio of learning. This is a method of determining the average reading growth per month of schooling for each child, first, prior to admission to a special reading service (remedial or reading clinic) and, later, whenever a testing program is desired. The first step is to compare for each pupil the reading grade score with the "grade equivalent" of the pupil. If the boy or girl has been held back once or more than once, the time for such repetitions of grades should be added to his "grade equivalent" to determine the expected achievement. Thus, if a pupil is in the third month of grade three, which he is repeating at the time, his expected reading achievement in grade score should be 4.3 (3.3 + 1.0). If his obtained reading grade score is 2.8 (the equivalent of eight months through grade two) it is these latter scores which are to be compared. For example, when the pupil actually achieves 2.8, he has theoretically learned 1.8 years in reading (2.8 — 1.0). This is so because all test scores start with 1.0. Actually this boy or girl should have achieved 3.3 grades in the course of his 4.3 years of instruction (4.3 — 1.0). The ratio between 1.8 and 3.3, or 0.55, represents the average reading growth per month which has occurred for this pupil prior to any special reading assistance.

Similarly, such ratios may be obtained for all the pupils in any caseload of remedial reading or reading clinic program; and these percentages will represent, roughly, their learning efficiency at the time of acceptance into the special reading program. When an evaluation is made, each pupil's total reading test score may be converted to a grade score. If the efficiency with which he has responded to the reading program is to be compared with his original ratio, the difference between the two scores must be divided by the months of special service provided.

For example, if the pupil who began with a reading grade score of 2.8 reached a grade score of 4.5 after 1.4 years of instruction, his average ratio of growth during the period of special reading service is obtained by dividing the gain (4.5 — 2.8) or 1.7 years or 17 months by 14 months (the length of service) to obtain 121% or an average of 1.21 months of grade score per month of instruction. This figure represents a considerable gain over the 0.55 months which was characteristic of the pupil upon admission to this special reading program (remedial or reading clinic). If such figures are available for all the pupils, they may be dealt with by various statistical procedures to show the changes in learning efficiency. The data may be totaled and/or separated into subgroups by grade groups, by teaching caseloads, or by groups having been provided with varying lengths of service, and the scores distributed so that central tendencies can be ascertained. For example, in the New York City Special Reading Services program, the statistics for the 1964–65 school year showed at the close of the school term an average reading growth per month of 120 percent. The same pupils upon entering this program had had an average reading growth of only 43 percent per month. These are rather easily understood, meaningful figures which can be given to school personnel and even to the public in general, who may want to know if a special reading program actually results in pupils' improved learning. (For further details, see Appendix A.)

7.4   YEAR-END EVALUATION— ACCURACY RATINGS

Another way of evaluating the reading growth of pupils after a period of special instruction is to note the reduction in errors made on silent reading tests. This is achieved by obtaining "reading accuracy ratings." These "accuracy ratings" are based on the number of correct items divided by the number of attempted items. The New York Tests of Growth in Reading provide these ratings but they can be worked out readily. Initial versus final reading results may be evaluated by comparing these "accuracy ratings" in terms of the percentages obtained at each testing period.

7.5   INTERIM OR YEAR-END EVALUATION—THE PARENT

Parents are another resource in the process of evaluation. The remedial reading teacher should schedule periodic conferences with the parent of each pupil receiving special instruction. During these conferences she will elicit from the parent specific answers to inquiries regarding evidences of the pupil's improvement in reading. For example, does he seem more interested in reading? Does he read more books? Does he ask his parents to read to him? Does he seem happier about school and himself? Are there any noticeable changes in his behavior?

For the pupil in the reading clinic, the social worker and/or the reading clinic teacher may gather such information from the parent. Further information may be elicited regarding personality adjustment, such as, does the pupil show increased ability to get along with siblings—with playmates? Does the parent want to continue in the group program? If the parent is being seen by the social worker on an individual basis, inquiry should be made as to whether the parent feels this is helping her and she wants to continue in it.

While answers to these questions by the parents may be influenced somewhat by a parent's wishes, the general tenor of a parent's evaluation is likely to be fairly dependable, especially if her comments are compared with her report about her child and his reading problem at the first interview.

7.6   INTERIM OR YEAR-END EVALUATION—THE PUPIL

The children themselves may be asked to evaluate their own reading progress. This is done by checking written answers to questions phrased and read to them by their remedial reading or reading clinic teacher. The replies should be interpreted by teachers other than their own in order that they may be interpreted as objectively as possible. On the following page appears the form "Pupil's Estimate of His Progress in Reading."

7.7   INTERIM OR END-TERM EVALUATION— THE CLASSROOM TEACHER

The Form, "Class Teacher's Evaluation of Pupil Progress," appears on page 121. This form is to be completed by the pupil's class, English

PUPIL'S ESTIMATE OF HIS PROGRESS IN READING

Directions: Pupil is to check any statement which he considers to be true of him.
(These statements may be read to the pupil.)

I think that during the present school year

_____ I have learned more about reading than in any previous school year.

_____ I have gained as much in reading as I did last year.

_____ I have enjoyed reading more than ever before.

_____ I still have trouble with new words.

_____ My school marks are not as high as they used to be.

_____ My marks have improved

        _____ very much.

        _____ somewhat.

        _____ very little.

_____ I want to continue in the reading program.

Signed_____
(Pupil)

Grade_____

Teacher's Evaluation: Taking the above into account, the class teacher's report, and also the test results, check one of the following as representative of this pupil:

_____ No improvement

_____ Fair improvement

_____ Very good progress

_____ Excellent progress

Signed_____
(Remedial Reading Teacher or
Reading Clinic Teacher)

Checked by_____

CLASS TEACHER'S EVALUATION OF PUPIL PROGRESS

Name of Pupil_____Date_____

School_____Class_____Teacher_____

1. To what extent does this child participate in classroom activities?

   In what area does (he, she) have the most difficulty?

2. What is (his, her) relationship to other members of (his, her) class?

3. What is (his, her) attitude toward authority? toward necessary rules and regulations?

   Does (he, she) seek special attention from the teacher?

4. What other special problems exist?

5. What is your estimate of the pupil's present reading level?

6. What special problems, if any, does the pupil present in reading?

7. Has the pupil's attitude toward reading improved?

and/or homeroom teacher at interim or end-term evaluation periods. In addition, there should be periodic evaluations with the pupil's class, English and/or homeroom teacher during scheduled conferences.

7.8 INTERIM OR END-TERM EVALUATION—THE SUPERVISOR

Principals of referring schools should be asked to evaluate the program in writing through answers to questions such as, "To what extent has pupil shown evidence of growth in reading and other curriculum areas? Do the class teachers indicate that they have received help through consultations with the staff or through demonstration lessons by the reading specialist? Have they observed changes in the behavior of the pupils?" It is well also to allow for negative criticism by asking directly if there are suggestions for improvement of the service. In addition, evaluative conferences should be held with the superintendent.

These evaluative procedures are based on the experiences of the authors working with reading specialists. These procedures seek to include the child, the parent, the class teacher, the principal and the usual measurement, the testing program. The ratio of learning and the "reading accuracy rating" are somewhat different, more detailed, and meaningful to professional and lay people.

APPENDIX A
SUMMARY STATISTICS

The statistics that appear on the following pages and the investigations summarized are the most recent figures obtained in the Reading Clinics under the direction of one of the authors.* As will be noted, the first page of figures pertains to facts concerning the total group of pupils who were serviced by the eleven clinics in this program. These numbered 3,098 boys and girls, who attended 83 elementary schools located in the five boroughs of New York City. (See Table I.)

On the official caseloads were 1,350 pupils who, after diagnostic study, received instructional help on a regular basis and clinical services as needed; 671 were on the provisional caseloads (usually sixth grade pupils who were given short term reading diagnosis and instruction to facilitate their readiness for promotion to junior high schools) and 112 were "follow-up" cases. The latter had been "promoted" from the official caseloads and were continued for less frequent reading instruction and guidance in order to insure that previously indicated reading growth and personal-social development would be maintained. An additional 965 pupils, also referred by the schools, received only partial service, usually reading diagnosis and a brief clinical evaluation. Some of these boys and girls moved out of the district; some

*These are the most recently available statistics for the New York City Elementary Reading Clinics. They are based on the work of the year 1964–65.

were still in the process of selection and would be accepted for full service later; and a few were not accepted for a number of different reasons.

Directly participating in the work of the Reading Clinics were the 622 classroom teachers of the children who received help from the reading clinics. This work entailed frequent conferences with reading clinic teachers, psychologists and psychiatric social workers. In special cases recommendations of the psychiatrists were also communicated to school personnel.

Comparison between these 1965 statistics and those reported in 1964 is of interest. The total official caseload for the past year increased by approximately one hundred children, and the provisional caseload also increased by 132 cases. The number of children given follow-up service was again somewhat higher than in previous years.

In the total official caseload, boys continued to outnumber girls and to a somewhat greater extent than in 1964. The boys represent 68% of the total and the girls 32%. In the provisional caseload, however, this sex difference is not maintained—the number of boys and girls being almost equal. It would appear that, whereas the acute symptom of reading difficulty as found in the primary and early elementary grades characterizes many more boys than girls, there may be an equal proportion of the two sexes in the later elementary grades who lag somewhat behind grade standards in reading achievement, presenting a variety of less severe learning difficulties. The latter respond well to the relatively brief program offered to them as provisional cases by the Reading Clinics, as will be noted from the data given on the following pages.

TABLE I. SCOPE OF READING CLINICS

Total number of children serviced	Boys	Girls	Total
Official Caseload	919	431	1350
Provisional Caseload	348	323	671
Follow-up Group Alumni	80	32	112
Partial Service			965
Grand Total			**3098**
Schools Serviced Schools in five boroughs serviced by 11 Reading Clinics			83
Total number of classroom teachers participating directly in the program			622

TABLE II. READING ACHIEVEMENT ON ADMISSION COMPARED WITH RESULTS IN MAY 1965

	READING ACHIEVEMENT ON ADMISSION		READING ACHIEVEMENT, MAY 1965	
	Range of Grade Scores	Medians	Range of Grade Scores	Medians
Official Caseload				
Boys	*n.r.–4.3	2.4	1.5–8.0	3.8
Girls	n.r.–3.9	2.5	1.7–6.5	3.9
Total	n.r.–4.3	2.4	1.5–8.0	3.8
Provisional Caseload				
Boys	1.8–5.2	4.0	2.0–9.2	5.0
Girls	2.0–5.3	4.1	3.0–7.7	5.2
Total	1.8–5.3	4.0	2.0–9.2	5.1
Follow-up Group				
Boys	*n.r.–3.9	2.7	4.8–11.0+	6.7
Girls	1.8–3.6	2.8	5.1–9.2	6.3
Total	n.r.–3.9	2.6	4.8–11.0+	6.8

*n.r. non-reader

TABLE III. READING RETARDATION AT BEGINNING OF SERVICE

Reading Retardation in Years	Official Caseload			Provisional Caseload			Follow-up Group		
	Boys	Girls	Total	Boys	Girls	Total	Boys	Girls	Total
5.6–6.5	6		6						
4.6–5.5	2	1	3	7		7			
3.6–4.5	23	7	30	16	7	23			
2.6–3.5	151	47	198	75	69	144	6	1	7
1.6–2.5	486	219	705	208	197	405	35	19	54
.6–1.5	250	157	407	41	49	90	39	11	50
Below .6	1		1	1	1	2		1	1
Totals	**919**	**431**	**1350**	**348**	**323**	**671**	**80**	**32**	**112**
Median Retardation	2.0	1.8	1.9	2.2	2.1	2.2	1.6	1.8	1.6

TABLE IV. READING IMPROVEMENT SHOWN BY MAY 1965 TESTS

Reading Gain in Years	Official Caseload			Provisional Caseload			Follow-up Group		
	Boys	Girls	Total	Boys	Girls	Total	Boys	Girls	Total
8.6–9.5							1		1
7.6–8.5							4		4
6.6–7.5	1		1				2	2	4
5.6–6.5	2		2				8	3	11
4.6–5.5	6	1	7	1		1	13	7	20
3.6–4.5	35	12	47	5	2	7	20	5	25
2.6–3.5	121	53	174	11	13	24	28	12	40
1.6–2.5	181	101	282	77	83	160	3	2	5
.6–1.5	332	172	504	171	162	333			
.1–0.5	133	55	188	48	37	85			
0	14	1	15	5	3	8			
Regressed	15	1	16	7	2	9			
Transferred absent not tested	79	35	114	23	21	44	1	1	2
Totals	**919**	**431**	**1350**	**348**	**323**	**671**	**80**	**32**	**112**
Median Gain in Reading	1.3	1.4	1.3	1.2	1.2	1.2	4.0	3.9	4.0
Median Length of Service	1.0	1.1	1.0	.4	.4	.4			

Table II shows that girls in the official caseload do not score quite so low in reading as the boys. This fact is indicated by their higher median grade score (2.5 versus 2.4) obtained at the time of admission to the program and also on the most recent test in May 1965 (3.9 versus 3.8). Though these sex differences in medians may appear slight, they are considered significant in view of the fact that they are based upon such large caseloads.

Tables III and IV show in more detail initial retardation in reading and reading gains. The reading retardation of each child at the beginning of service was determined by substracting his actual reading grade score from his grade placement. In the official caseload, by far the largest number of cases falls between one and a half and two and a half years' retardation. The median retardation of the official caseload on admission was 1.9 years (the girls' 1.8 and the boys' 2.0).

TABLE V. MEDIANS OF READING GROWTH
INDICES FOR THE ELEVEN CLINICS

Clinic	PRIOR TO ADMISSION		SINCE ADMISSION	
	Official Caseload	Provisional Caseload	Official Caseload	Provisional Caseload
1.	.43	.57	1.20	2.00
2.	.34	.56	1.41	4.00
3.	.39	.55	1.14	2.66
4.	.41	.62	1.00	1.75
5.	.44	.55	1.60	3.25
6.	.50	.59	1.38	3.67
7.	.46	.56	1.29	2.75
8.	.42	.63	1.14	2.00
9.	.42	.65	1.03	1.63
10.	.47	.60	1.17	3.00
11.	.42	None	1.17	None

Explanation: Expected growth in reading assumes a norm of 100%; e.g., a child attending school in the third month of the fourth grade should theoretically have acquired 3.3 years of reading score (4.3 − 1.0) in the 3.3 years attended and have "normal" reading growth of one month for each month of school attendance. An example of a retarded reader in the same school grade whose reading score was only 2.4 would have shown an average growth of only .42 per month "prior to admission" to the Reading Clinics.

$$\text{The method :} \quad \frac{2.4 - 1.0}{4.3 - 1.0} \quad \text{or} \quad \frac{1.4}{3.3} \quad \text{or} \quad .42$$

The reading gain for each pupil, computed by subtracting the original reading score from that obtained in May 1965, is then divided by the length of time the child has been in the Reading Clinics; and this provides the average reading growth per month "since admission" to the Reading Clinics. This pupil, who entered with a reading score of 2.4, achieved a score of 3.9 in May 1965.

$$\text{Example of a typical case:} \quad \frac{3.9 - 2.4}{1.2} \quad \text{or} \quad \frac{1.5}{1.2} \quad \text{or} \quad 1.25$$

Reading gains made by the 1,236 "official" pupils who were tested in May 1965 ranged widely, with the median at 1.3 years. When it is realized that the median length of service of the official caseload was only 1.0 year, it is evident that these pupils made notable progress. The children in the provisional caseload who, it will be recalled, were older and typically characterized by fourth grade rather than sixth grade reading ability, made very rapid growth in a short time, gaining 1.2 years in four months' time (medians).

In the next tabulation (Table V), dramatic changes are shown in the reading growth indices of the pupils following their admission to the Reading Clinics. In each of the eleven clinics, the average reading growth per month of school instruction was computed for every pupil at the time of his admission to this program and again in May 1965. For both the official and provisional caseloads of every clinic, the medians were obtained of these reading growth indices prior to admission and since admission. Examination of Table V, will show, first, the extent of the learning difficulties in reading of the pupils prior to their admission to the Reading Clinic program. The medians of the reading growth per month had been .50 or lower in all official caseloads of the eleven clinics. According to reading tests given in May 1965 the corresponding medians were 1.00 or higher in all the clinics. In some cases the medians based on recent tests were three times as high as those for the same children prior to their admission to the Reading Clinics. As might be assumed from information given previously about provisional caseloads, they had higher growth rates prior to admission and, in general, increased even more rapidly following Reading Clinic service.

Some of the favorable changes which occur in the children's attitudes toward reading can be inferred from the evidence of their improved work habits on silent reading tests. The next section of this report which deals with Changes in Accuracy Ratings presents a discussion of this factor and then gives statistical data for May 1965.

The manual for Test B of the New York Tests of Growth in Reading, the test which is often used with pupils before admission to the Reading Clinics, states the following regarding "Accuracy Ratings":

... Their Meaning. It has been found that children at this stage of reading differ significantly not only in their grades scores (based on the number of items correct) but also in the proportionate amount of error which characterizes their work on silent reading tests. If a child is able to read a selection or most of a selection, he will usually attempt to answer all the questions concerning it. He will mark the items which he thinks he understands and also those of which he feels somewhat uncertain. When not enough of a selection can be read for test items to be comprehended, some children will resort to guessing whereas others will omit those items. Extremes in both directions—rash guessing or excessive caution—are undesirable. Particularly when children are still in the formative stage in developing reading habits, it is desirable for the teacher to know what tendencies to accuracy or inaccuracy characterize the reading habits of her pupils.

Reference to Table VI and to the graph following Table VI show characteristic results for pupils before and after instruction in the Reading Clinics. On admission a very high proportion of the students obtain "Very Low" and "Low" accuracy ratings (totals of 42% and 32% respectively, by comparison with norms of only 25% and 15%). In general, these are the boys and girls who do not look upon themselves as capable of making progress in reading. They are ill at ease during a test and "act out" by marking at random when they cannot read the material, rather than show the Reading Clinic teacher or the other pupils that they can do very little reading. After a time in the Reading Clinics, even when there has not yet been a long enough period of instruction for the pupils to gain a great deal in terms of grade score, there is an appreciable change in the accuracy ratings obtained—whether on the same test or on a harder test. After the pupils accept their reading problem frankly, and begin to gain confidence that they are capable of learning, they approach a test quite differently. The "rash guessing" is reduced markedly—even below expectancy for a

TABLE VI. ACCURACY RATINGS ON INITIAL AND END-OF-TERM READING TESTS* COMPARED WITH TEST NORMS**

Accuracy Ratings	Test Results On Admission			Test Results May 1965			Test Norms
	Boys %	Girls %	Total %	Boys %	Girls %	Total %	%
Very High	4	3	4	19	15	18	25
High	11	14	12	23	28	25	15
Medium	10	10	10	27	28	27	20
Low	30	37	32	19	22	20	15
Very Low	45	36	42	12	7	10	25
Total %	100	100	100	100	100	100	100
Number of Children	818	388	1,206	818	388	1,206	

*New York tests of Growth in Reading—Tests B, C or D.

**The 1206 children tested (818 boys and 388 girls) are all those on the official caseloads of the eleven clinics except those for whom Accuracy Ratings were not obtainable on the initial test, those newly admitted to the program and absentees from the 1965 testing.

normal population. There is more than four times the percentage in the category of "Very High" accuracy and better than doubling of the percentages of those pupils who reach "High" and "Medium" accuracy.

IMPROVEMENT IN ACCURACY OF READING OF 1206 PUPILS IN THE READING CLINICS

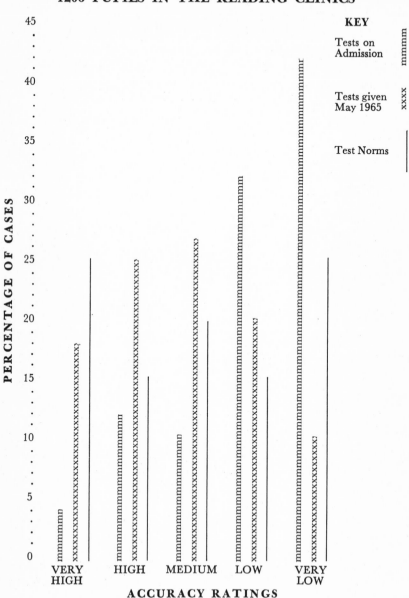

ACCURACY RATINGS

The chart opposite shows the percentage distribution of Accuracy Ratings (Very High, High, Medium, Low, Very Low) of pupils tested on admission to the Reading Clinics and in May 1965. For comparative purposes the test norms for accuracy are also shown. The tests used were N.Y. Growth in Reading—Test B, C or D, depending upon each pupil's reading ability at the time of testing. The boys and girls tested were all those on the official caseload of the eleven clinics except those for whom accuracy could not be measured on the initial test, those newly admitted to the program, and those who were absent for the May 1965 testing.

The above data were also tallied separately for boys and girls (See Table VI) and no significant sex differences were found. Though girls, in general, make up a smaller proportion of pupils requiring clinical service, those who have serious reading difficulties resemble the boys—at least in attitude toward reading and poor work habits as reflected in their "Accuracy Ratings."

The great reduction in errors made on the recent tests shown graphically points to the probability that these gains in accuracy reflect not only increased skills in silent reading but also gains in personal well-being. The pupils who receive service in the Reading Clinics are thought to experience a reduction in anxiety regarding reading and a corresponding increase in self-confidence with regard to their own learning efforts. In producing these favorable results, the specialized instruction of the reading clinic teacher has undoubtedly been made more effective by the work of other members of the clinic team.

APPENDIX B
PROFESSIONAL BIBLIOGRAPHY

This list of professional books on reading has been found useful by teachers, supervisors, and reading specialists with whom the authors have worked.

Austin, Mary C. *The Torchlighters.* Cambridge, Massachusetts: Harvard University Press, 1961.

Austin, Mary C., Coleman Morrison, and others. *The First R: The Harvard Report on Reading in Elementary Schools.* New York: Macmillan Co., 1963.

Austin, Mary C., Clifford L. Bush, and Mildred H. Huebner. *Reading Evaluation: Appraisal Techniques for School and Classroom.* New York: Ronald Press, 1961.

Betts, Emmett A. *Foundations of Reading Instruction.* New York: American Book Co., 1957.

Bloomfield, L. and C. Barnhart. *Let's Read: A Linguistic Approach.* Detroit: Wayne State University Press, 1961.

Bond, Guy L. and Miles A. Tinker. *Reading Difficulties: Their Diagnosis and Correction.* New York: Appleton-Century-Crofts, Inc., 1957.

Bond, Guy L. and Eva Bond Wagner. *Teaching the Child to Read,* fourth edition. New York: Macmillan Co., 1966.

Botel, Morton. *How to Teach Reading.* State College, Pennsylvania: Penn Valley Publishing Co., 1959.

Bureau of Educational Research. *A Practical Guide to Individualized Reading,* Publication No. 40. City of New York, Board of Education, October 1960.

Burton, W. H., C. Baker, and G. Kemp. *Reading in Child Development.* Indianapolis: Bobbs-Merrill Co., 1956.

Causey, Oscar S., ed. *The Reading Teacher's Reader.* New York: Ronald Press, 1958.

Chall, Jeanne. *Readability: An Appraisal of Research Application,* Monograph No. 34, Bureau of Educational Research. Columbus, Ohio: Ohio State University, 1958.

Cutts, W. G., ed. *Teaching Young Children to Read: Proceedings of a Conference, November 14–16, 1962.* Washington, D. C.: U. S. Department of Health, Education, and Welfare. Office of Education.

Dawson, Mildred A. and Harry A. Bamman. *Fundamentals of Basic Reading Instruction.* New York: Longmans, Green & Company, 1959.

DeBoer, John J. and Martha Dallman. *The Teaching of Reading,* revised edition. New York: Holt, Rinehart and Winston, Inc., 1964.

Dolch, Edward W. *Teaching Primary Reading,* third edition. Champaign, Illinois: Garrard Press, 1960.

_____. *A Manual for Remedial Reading,* second edition. Champaign, Illinois: Garrard Press, 1945.

Durrell, Donald D. *Improving Reading Instruction.* New York: World Book Co., 1956.

Ephron, B. K. *Emotional Difficulties in Reading.* New York: Julian Press, 1953.

Fernald, Grace M. *Remedial Techniques in Basic School Subjects.* New York: McGraw-Hill Book Co., 1943.

Figurel, J. Allen, ed. *Reading and Inquiry,* International Reading Association Conference Proceedings, Vol. 10. Newark, Delaware: The Association, 1965.

_____. *Improvement of Reading Through Classroom Practice,* I. R. A. Conference Proceedings, Vol. 9. Newark, Delaware: The Association, 1964.

_____. *Reading as an Intellectual Activity,* I. R. A. Conference Proceedings, Vol. 8. Newark, Delaware: The Association, 1963.

_____. *Challenge and Experiment in Reading,* I. R. A. Conference Proceedings, Vol. 7. Newark, Delaware: The Association, 1962.

Gans, Roma. *Common Sense in Teaching Reading.* Indianapolis: Bobbs-Merrill Co., 1963.

Gates, Arthur I. *Reading Attainment in Elementary Schools, 1957 and 1937.* New York: Bureau of Publications, Teachers College, Columbia University, 1961.

──────── *A Reading Vocabulary for the Primary Grades.* New York: Bureau of Publications, Teachers College, Columbia University, 1955.

──────── *The Improvement of Reading: A Program of Diagnostic and Remedial Methods,* third edition. New York: Macmillan Co., 1947.

Gray, William S. *On Their Own in Reading,* revised edition. Fairlawn, New Jersey: Scott, Foresman and Co., 1960.

Gray, William S. and Bernice Rogers. *Maturity in Reading: Its Nature and Appraisal.* Chicago: University of Chicago Press, 1956.

Harris, Albert J. *Readings on Reading Instruction.* New York: David McKay Co., Inc., 1963.

──────── *How to Increase Reading Ability: A Guide to Developmental and Remedial Methods,* fourth edition, revised. New York: Longmans, Green & Company, 1961.

Heilman, Arthur W. *Principles and Practices of Teaching Reading.* Columbus, Ohio: Charles E. Merrill Books, Inc., 1961.

Hester, Kathleen B. *Teaching Every Child to Read,* second edition. New York: Harper and Row, 1964.

Hildreth, Gertrude. *Teaching Reading.* New York: Henry Holt and Co., 1958.

International Reading Association. *Invitational Addresses, 1965, Tenth Annual Convention.* Newark, Delaware: The Association, 1965.

Karlin, Robert. *Teaching Reading in High School.* Indianapolis, Indiana: Bobbs-Merrill Co., 1964.

Kottmeyer, William. *Teacher's Guide for Remedial Reading.* St. Louis, Missouri: Webster Publishing Co., 1959.

──────── *Handbook for Remedial Reading.* St. Louis, Missouri: Webster Publishing Co., 1947.

Larrick, Nancy. *A Parent's Guide to Children's Books.* Columbus, Ohio: Charles E. Merrill Books, Inc., 1960.

──────── *A Teacher's Guide to Children's Books.* Garden City, New York: Doubleday and Co., 1958.

Learning to Read: A Report of a Conference of Reading Experts. Foreword by James B. Conant. Princeton, New Jersey: Educational Testing Service, 1962.

Lee, Dorris M. and R. V. Allen. *Learning to Read Through Experience.* New York: Appleton-Century-Crofts, Inc., 1963.

Mazurkiewicz, Albert J., ed. *New Perspectives in Reading Instruction: A Book of Readings.* New York: Pitman Publishing Corp., 1964.

McKee, Paul. *The Teaching of Reading in the Elementary School.* Boston: Houghton Mifflin Co., 1948.

McKim, M. G. and H. Caskey. *Guiding Growth in Reading in the Modern Elementary School.* New York: Macmillan Co., 1963.

National Society for the Study of Education. *Sixtieth Yearbook, Part I: Development In and Through Reading.* Chicago: University of Chicago Press, 1961.

_____. *Forty-eighth Yearbook, Part II: Reading in the Elementary School.* Chicago: University of Chicago Press, 1949.

_____. *Forty-seventh Yearbook, Part II: Reading in the High School and College.* Chicago: University of Chicago Press, 1948.

Orton, Samuel T. *Reading, Writing and Speech Problems in Children.* New York: W. W. Norton and Co., 1961.

Robinson, H. Alan, ed. *Recent Developments in Reading,* Supplementary Monograph: SEM 95. Chicago: University of Chicago Press, 1965.

_____. *Meeting Individual Difficulties in Reading,* Supplementary Monograph: SEM 94. Chicago: University of Chicago Press, 1964.

_____. *The Underachiever in Reading,* Supplementary Monograph: SEM 92. Chicago: University of Chicago Press, 1962.

Robinson, Helen M. *Why Pupils Fail in Reading.* Chicago: University of Chicago Press, 1946.

Roswell, F. and G. Natchez. *Reading Disability: Diagnosis and Treatment.* New York: Basic Books, Inc., 1964.

Russell, David H. *Children Learn to Read.* Boston: Ginn and Co., 1961.

Russell, David H. and Etta E. Karp. *Reading Aids Through the Grades,* revised. New York: Bureau of Publications, Teachers College, Columbia University, 1951.

Smith, Nila B. *American Reading Instruction.* Newark, Delaware: International Reading Association, 1963.

_____. *Reading Instruction for Today's Children.* Englewood Cliffs, New Jersey: Prentice-Hall, Inc., 1963.

_____. *Read Faster and Get More from Your Reading.* Englewood Cliffs, New Jersey: Prentice-Hall, Inc., 1958.

Spache, George D. *Toward Better Reading.* Champaign, Illinois: Garrard Press, 1963.

_____. *Good Reading for Poor Readers.* Champaign, Illinois: Garrard Press, 1962.

Strang, R. and D. K. Bracken. *Making Better Readers.* Boston: D. C. Heath and Co., 1957.

Strang, R., C. M. McCullough, and A. E. Traxler. *The Improvement of Reading,* third edition. New York: McGraw-Hill Book Co., 1961.

Tinker, M. A. and C. McCullough. *Teaching Elementary Reading,* second edition. New York: Appleton-Century-Crofts, Inc., 1963.

University of the State of New York. *Report of Regents Conference on the Improvement of Reading.* Albany: State Education Department, 1962.

Veatch, Jeannette. *Individualizing Your Reading Program: Self-Selection in Action.* New York: G. P. Putnam's Sons, 1959.

Vernon, Magdalene D. *Backwardness in Reading: A Study of Its Nature and Origin.* Cambridge: Cambridge University Press, 1957.

Weiss, M. Jerry. *Reading in the Secondary Schools.* New York: Odyssey Press, 1961.

Witty, Paul A. *How to Improve Your Reading.* Chicago: Science Research Associates, 1956.

------------. *Reading in Modern Education.* Boston: D. C. Heath and Co., 1949.

Woolf, M. D. and J. A. Woolf. *Remedial Reading: Teaching and Treatment.* New York: McGraw-Hill Book Co., 1957.

Yoakam, Gerald A. *Basal Reading Instruction.* New York: McGraw-Hill Book Co., 1955.

APPENDIX C
LISTS OF BOOKS

The list of books that follow have proven to be of special value for pupils on the grade levels indicated. These levels are easily converted for use in schools organized on a non-graded basis.

GRADES 1–3

Author	Title	Publisher
Adams	First Things	Platt
Adelson	All Ready for Summer	McKay
Adelson	All Ready for Winter	McKay
Agle	Three Boys and a Helicopter	Scribner
Aldis	Cindy	Putnam
Alexander	ABC of Cars and Trucks	Doubleday
Alleyne	Story of Sammy Sticklepin	Warne
Anderson, C.	Blaze and the Gypsies	Macmillan
Anderson, C.	Linda and the Indians	Macmillan
Anderson, H.	The Steadfast Tin Soldier	Scribner
Anglund	The Brave Cowboy	Harcourt
Ardizzone	Tim All Alone	Walck
Assoc. for Child. Ed.	Told Under the Blue Umbrella	Macmillan
Austin	William's Shadow	Dutton
Averill	Jenny's Birthday Book	Harper

Author	Title	Publisher
Ballard	The True Book of Reptiles	Children's
Bannon	Billy and the Bear	Houghton
Barr	Fireman Fred	Whitman
Barr	Texas Pete, Little Cowboy	Whitman
Beatty	Little Owl Indian	Houghton
Beatty	Little Wild Horse	Houghton
Behn	All Kinds of Time	Harcourt
Beim	Mister Boss	Morrow
Beim	Smallest Boy In the Class	Morrow
Bell	Wanted: A Brother	Abingdon
Bemelmans	Madeline and the Bad Hat	Simon
Bemelmans	Madeline and the Gypsies	Viking
Berkley	Ups and Downs	Scott
Bishop	The Five Chinese Brothers	Hale
Bishop	The Man Who Lost His Head	Viking
Black	Dusty and His Friends	Hale
Blumenthal	Tit For Tat Tommy	Oxford
Branley	Book of Moon Rockets	Crowell
Branley	Mickey's Magnet	Crowell
Bridges	Zoo Babies	Morrow
Bright	Georgie	Doubleday
Bright	Georgie To the Rescue	Doubleday
Brock	Skipping Island	Knopf
Bromhall	Mary Ann's First Picture	Knopf
Brown	The Little Brass Band	Harper
Brown	Wheel On the Chimney	Doubleday
Bryant	Let's Be Friends	Children's
Buff	Elf Owl	Viking
Buff	Hurry, Skurry and Flurry	Viking
Bulla	Ghost Town Treasure	Crowell
Bulla	Poppy Seeds	Crowell
Burgess	Goops and How To Be Them	Lippincott
Burton	Maybelle the Cable Car	Houghton
Burton	Mike Mulligan and the Steam Shovel	Houghton
Carmichael	Lee Fong and His Toy Junk	McKay
Carroll	Where's the Bunny?	Oxford
Cassell	Fun Together	Broadman
Catling	The Chocolate Touch	Morrow
Caudill	Schoolroom In the Parlor	Winston

Author	Title	Publisher
Cerf	Bennett Cerf's Book of Riddles	Random
Chandler	Cowboy Sam and the Rustlers	Benefic
Child Study Assn.	Read To Me Again	Crowell
Ciardi	I Met a Man	Houghton
Clewes	The Happiest Day	Coward
Corcos	Joel Gets a Haircut	Abelard
Creekmore	Fujio	Hale
D'Aulaire	Abraham Lincoln	Doubleday
D'Aulaire	Nils	Doubleday
Davis	Timothy Turtle	Hale
De Angeli	Thee, Hannah	Doubleday
Dennis	Flip and the Morning	Viking
De Regniers	A Child's Book of Dreams	Harcourt
Dobbs	Once Upon a Time	Random
Doss	Friends Around the World	Abingdon
Dougherty	Andy and the Lion	Hale
Dow	My Time of Year	Walck
Downer	The Flower	Scott
Duvoisin	A Is For the Ark	Lothrop
Duvoisin	Petunia	Knopf
Earle	My Friend Johnny	Lothrop
Eastman	Sam and the Firefly	Random
Eberle	The Very Good Neighbors	Lippincott
Eichenberg	Ape In a Cape	Harcourt
Elking	Big Jump	Random
Embry	Blue-Nosed Witch	Holiday
Erickson	Slip, the Story of a Little Fox	Hale
Estes	Little Oven	Harcourt
Ets	Another Day	Viking
Fatio	The Happy Lion	McGraw
Felt	Rosa-Too-Little	Doubleday
Fisher	Runny Days, Sunny Days	Abelard
Flack	Angus and the Cat	Doubleday
Flack	Angus Lost	Doubleday
Francoise	Biquette the White Goat	Scribner
Frederick	Cloud Hoppers	Children's
Freeman	Space Witch	Viking
Friedrick	The Marshmallow Ghosts	Lothrop

Author	Title	Publisher
Friskey	Mystery of the Broken Bridge	Children's
Funk	I Read Signs	Holiday
Gag	The ABC Bunny	Hale
Geisel	Horton Hatches an Egg	Hale
Goudey	Good Rain	Dutton
Gramatky	Little Toot	Hale
Gramatky	Loopy	Hale
Green	Everybody Eats	Scott
Haywood	"B" Is for "Betsy"	Harcourt
Hoberman	All My Shoes Come In Two's	Little
Hoder	Big City	Macmillan
Hoff	Eight Little Artists	Abelard
Hogan	Bear Is a Bear	Dutton
Hogner	Sad Eye the Clown	Hale
Holland	A Tree for Teddy	Knopf
Humphreys	The Big Book of Animals Every Child Should Know	Grosset
Hunt	The Double Birthday Present	Lippincott
Hurd	Benny the Bulldozer	Lothrop
Ilsley	The Pink Hat	Lippincott
Ipcar	One Horse Farm	Doubleday
Jacobs	Toy Shop Mystery	Coward
Jerrold	Swimming Hole	Morrow
Johnson, E.	Three-In-One Prince	Little
Johnson, M.	Gay: A Shetland Sheep Dog	Morrow
Kahl	Away Went Wolfgang	Scribner
Kamerman	Little Plays for Little Players	Plays
Kayt	The Magic Mitt	Hastings
Kepes	Beasts From a Brush	Pantheon
King	The Biggest Hat In the World	Dutton
Kingman	Peter's Long Walk	Doubleday
Koch	I Play At the Beach	Hale
Krauss	A Hole Is To Dig	Harper
Kravetz	Two For a Walk	Oxford

Author	Title	Publisher
Lansing	Being Nice Is Lots of Fun	Hart
Lattimore	Indigo Hill	Morrow
Lawson	Edward, Happy and Joe	Hale
Leaf	Manners Can Be Fun	Lippincott
Lenski	We Live In the City	Lippincott
Lexau	Olaf Reads	Dial
Lindop	Jumbo, King of the Elephants	Little
Lipkind	Circus Ruckus	Harcourt
Mandel	Make Your Own Musical Instruments	Sterling
Martin	Lightning, A Cowboy's Colt	Winston
Mason	Hominy and His Blunt-Nosed Arrow	Macmillan
Mattil	Meaning In Crafts	Prentice
McClintock	Fly Went By	Random
McCloskey	Make Way For Ducklings	Viking
McClung	Major: The Story of a Black Bear	Morrow
McGinley	The Most Wonderful Doll In the World	Lippincott
McGreal	Andy the Musical Ant	Dutton
Miles	Cooking Book	Knopf
Miner	The True Story of Plants We Know	Children's
Moore	Important Pockets of Paul	Hale
Moore	Old Rosie, the Horse Nobody Understood	Hale
Moran	Miserable	Bobbs
Morrow	Painted Pig	Knopf
Morton	Rags, the Fire House Dog	Winston
Newberry	Marshmallow	Harper
Oliver	Rain or Shine Things To Make	Harcourt
Otteson	Big Dog Tiny	Exposition
Otto	Little Old Train	Knopf
Palazzo	Frederico, the Flying Squirrel	Viking
Parkin	The Red Carpet	Macmillan
Patton	Little House On Stilts	Whitman
Pease	This Is Our Land	Rand
Penn	Mommies Are For Loving	Putnam

Author	Title	Publisher
Petersham	The Box With Red Wheels	Macmillan
Phelan	The White House	Holt
Pine	Air All Around	McGraw
Pine	The Indians Knew	McGraw
Podendorf	The True Book of Animal Babies	Children's
Potter	Ginger and Pickles	Warne
Preston	Smokey's Big Discovery	Walck
Purcell	The True Book of Holidays and Special Days	Children's
Rapaport	Whittle Too Much	Putnam
Rey	Cecily G. and the Nine Monkeys	Houghton
Rey	Pretzel	Harper
Reyner	My Mother Is the Most Beautiful Woman In the World	Lothrop
Rickert	The Bojabi Tree	Doubleday
Rose	Clara Barton	Garrard
Russell	From Rocks To Rockets	Rand
Sanders	Miranda the Panda is on the Veranda	Coward
Sattley	The Day the Empire State Went Visiting	Dodd
Schlein	A Bunny, A Bird, A Funny Cat	Abelard
Selden	I See What I See	Ariel
Seuss	If I Ran the Circus	Random
Shapp	Let's Find Out What Electricity Does	Watts
Shapp	Let's Find Out What's Light and What's Heavy	Watts
Slobodkin	Excuse Me! Certainly!	Vanguard
Slobodkin	Magic Michael	Macmillan
Spooner	Tony Plays With Sounds	Day
Steiner	Kiki Loves Music	Doubleday
Summers	Someone Else	Lippincott
Tarry	Hezekiah Horton	Viking
Taylor	Jasper the Drumming Boy	Viking
Tensen	Come To the Farm	Reilly
Thayer	Charley and the New Car	Morrow
Thorn	Let's Find Out	Benefic
Tousey	Cub Scout	Farrar
Tresselt	Autumn Harvest	Lothrop

Author	Title	Publisher
Uhl	About Cargo Ships	Melmont
Walkle	Adventures In Williamsburg	Colonial Williamsburg
Walters	The Steam Shovel That Wouldn't Eat Dirt	Dutton
Ward	The Biggest Bear	Houghton
Watson	When Is Tomorrow?	Knopf
Webb, A.	Birds In Their Homes	Doubleday
Webb, M.	Games For Younger Children	Morrow
Weir	Science, Science, Everywhere	Abingdon
Whiting	Negro Folk Tales	Associated
Witty	The True Book of Freedom and Our U.S. Family	Children's
Woolley	Railroad Cowboy	Morrow
Wright	Rainbow Dictionary	World
Wyndham	The Timid Dragon	Lothrop
Yashima	Plenty To Watch	Viking
Young	The Most Beautiful Kitten	Lantern
Zaffo	The Big Book of Real Boats and Ships	Grosset
Zim	Elephants	Morrow
Ziner	The True Book of Time	Children's
Zion	All Falling Down	Harper
Zolotow	Storm Book	Harper

GRADES 4–6

Author	Title	Publisher
Adler	Why? A Book of Reasons	Day
Adrian	Uranium Mystery	Hastings
Aesop	Fables	Walck
Allison	Helpful Helicopters	Melmont
Anderson	Junior Science Book of Sound	Garrard
Andrews	In the Days of the Dinosaurs	Random
Angelo	Big Little Island	Viking
Arnold	Sky Y Train	Broadman
Arnott	African Myths and Legends	Walck
Ashworth	Ten Pairs of Shoes	Friendship
Asimov	Satellites in Outer Space (rev.)	Random

Author	Title	Publisher
Ball	George Washington, First President	Abingdon
Banks	Mysterious Leaf	Harcourt
Batchelor	Communication: From Cave Writing To Television	Harcourt
Bate	Who Built the Bridge?	Scribner
Baum	Wizard of Oz	Reilly
Beals	Buffalo Bill	Wheeler
Behm	Two Uncles of Pablo	Harcourt
Beim	Laugh and Cry	Morrow
Bendick	First Book of Space Travel	Watts
Bethers	What Happens In the Sky	St. Martin's
Biemiller	Magic Ball From Mars	Morrow
Blough	Who Lives In This House?	McGraw
Borreson	Let's Go To an Art Museum	Putnam
Bowen	Stolen Spoon Mystery	Lippincott
Branley	Book of Astronauts For You	Crowell
Brenner	Bird In the Family	Scott
Brett	That Willy and Wally	Whitman
Brinton	Telephone	Day
Buck	Big Wave	Day
Buehr	Westward—With American Explorers	Putnam
Bulla	Riding the Pony Express	Crowell
Burt	Luther Burbank, Boy Wizard	Bobbs
Campbell	Nails To Nickels	Little
Carlson	Jokes and Riddles	Platt
Carmer	Henry Hudson	Garrard
Carroll	Alice in Wonderland	Random
Cathon	Perhaps and Perchance	Abingdon
Cervantes	Tales of Don Quixote and His Friends	Doubleday
Chandoha	All Kinds of Cats	Knopf
Chester	Let's Go On a Space Trip	Putnam
Christopher	Baseball Pals	Little
Chrystie	First Book of Surprising Facts	Watts
Clark	Thomas Alva Edison	Dutton
Colver	Florence Nightingale	Garrard
Corcoran	Elias Howe, Inventive Boy	Bobbs
Courlander	Piece of Fire and Other Haitian Tales	Harcourt
Cummings	101 Hand Puppets	McKay

Author	Title	Publisher
Daringer	Stepsister Sally	Harcourt
Darling	Sixty Million Years of Horses	Morrow
De Camp	Energy and Power	Golden
Defoe	Robinson Crusoe	Globe
De Leeuw	Salty Skinners	Little
Deucher	Young Brahms	Dutton
Deutsch	More Tales of Faraway Folk	Harper
Doane	Understanding Kim	Lippincott
Eager	Magic Or Not?	Harcourt
Edmonds	Ooka the Wise: Tales of Old Japan	Bobbs
Elgin	First Book of Mythology	Watts
Elliot	Singing Chameleon	Dufour
Elting	Trucks At Work	Harvey
Epstein	George Washington Carver	Garrard
Ericsson	About Glasses For Gladys	Leibel
Evans	All About Us	Golden
Fadiman	Story of Young King Arthur	Random
Fenton	Prehistoric Zoo	Doubleday
Feravolo	Junior Science Book of Heat	Garrard
Fox	Tasty Adventures in Science	Lantern
Freeman	Fun and Experiments With Light	Random
Freuchen	Eskimo Boy	Lothrop
Friedman	Ellen and the Gang	Morrow
Furman	Young Reader's Indian Stories	Grosset
Garelick	Manhattan Island	Crowell
Gee	Jeff and the River	Morrow
Georgiou	Wait and See	Harvey
Girl Scouts of America	Junior Girl Scout	Girl Scouts
Goldstein	Tools of the Scientist	Prentice
Gowan	Mystery of the Musical Umbrella	Random
Graham	Lafayette, Friend of America	Abingdon
Graves	Benjamin Franklin	Garrard
Greene	Trip On a Plane	Lantern
Grimm	Golden Bird and Other Fairy Tales	Macmillan
Grimm	Goose Girl	Doubleday

Author	Title	Publisher
Hall	World In a City Block	Viking
Hauff	Golden Treasury of Wonderful Fairy Tales	Golden
Hill	Wonderful Visit To Miss Liberty	Holt
Hinshaw	True Book of Your Body and You	Children's
Hodges	Three Princes of Serendip	Atheneum
Hoopes	What the President Does All Day	Day
Horgan	Toby and the Nighttime	Farrar
Howe	Amelia Earhart	Bobbs
Hughes	Dream Keep and Other Poems	Knopf
Hughes	First Book of Negroes	Watts
Hunt	Little Girl With Seven Names	Lippincott
Jackson	Little Major Leaguer	Hastings
Jagendorf	First Book of Puppets	Watts
Jane	Mystery Behind Dark Windows	Lippincott
Jupo	Nothing To Wear But Clothes	Dutton
Kaye	Around the World Story Book	Random
Kaye	Stories From Faraway Places	Random
Kirk	Lightning and the Rainbow	Follett
Kohn	Computers At Your Service	Prentice
Kroll	Young Medicine Man	Lantern
Lang	Blue Fairy Book	Longmans
Lang	Green Fairy Book	Longmans
Larrick	See For Yourself	Dutton
Larsen	Atoms and Atomic Energy	Day
Lauber	Story of Numbers	Random
LeGrand	How Basketball Began	Abingdon
Leaf	Geography Can Be Fun	Lippincott
Leavitt	True Book of Tools for Building	Children's
Lenski	Shoo-Fly Girl	Lippincott
Lewellen	Earth Satellite	Knopf
Lewis	Folding Paper Puppets	Lippincott
Lin	Milky Way and Other Chinese Folktales	Harcourt
Lipkind	Days To Remember	Obolensky
Loomis	All About Aviation	Random

Author	Title	Publisher
Lum	Holiday Moon	Abelard
Lyback	Indian Legends of the Great West	Lyons
MacKellar	Ghost In the Castle	McKay
Manning	Book of Dwarfs	Dutton
Margolis	Idy the Fox-Chasing Cow and Other Stories	World
Martin	John Fitzgerald Kennedy	Putnam
Mason	Dan Beard, Boy Scout	Bobbs
McCain	Writing	Farrar
McCloskey	Homer Price	Viking
McGinley	Boys Are Awful	Watts
McGovern	Why It's a Holiday	Random
McGuire	Daniel Boone	Wheeler
McMeekin	First Book of Horses	Watts
McNally	Fishing for Boys	Follett
Meyer	Machines	World
Milgrom	Science Book of Air Experiments	Science Materials
Miller	Make Way for Peggy O'Brien!	Lippincott
Monsell	Dolly Madison, Quaker Girl	Bobbs
Montgomery	Alexander Graham Bell	Garrard
Morton	Cooking Is Fun	Hart
Myrus	Astronauts	Grosset
Neurath	Wonder World of Snow and Ice	Lothrop
Oakes	Willy Wong, American	Messner
Parish	Let's Be Indians	Harper
Paul	Papa Luigi's Marionettes	Washburn
Peare	Louisa May Alcott, Her Life	Holt
Perrault	Complete Fairy Tales	Dodd
Pine	Chinese Knew	McGraw
Pine	Egyptians Knew	McGraw
Potter	Tongue Tanglers	World
Pringle	Young Edison	Roy
Prokofieff	Peter and the Wolf	Knopf
Pyle	Robin Hood	Scribner
Pyne	Little History of the United States	Houghton

Author	Title	Publisher
Radlauer	Good Times With Words	Melmont
Reck	First Book of Festivals Around the World	Watts
Rosenfield	Let's Go to Build the First Transcontinental Railroad	Putnam
Ruchlis	Thank You, Mr. Sun!	Harvey
Sasek	This Is New York	Macmillan
Sawyer	Enchanted Schoolhouse	Viking
Schloat	Your Wonderful Teeth	Scribner
Schneider	Let's Look Under the City	Scott
Schoor	Young John Kennedy	Harcourt
Schwartz	Earth Is Your Spaceship	McGraw
Seldon	Cricket In Times Square	Farrar
Selsam	See Through the Sea	Harper
Shields	Norah and the Cable Car	Longmans
Shotwell	Roosevelt Grady	World
Spicer	13 Monsters	Coward
Stevenson	George Carver, Boy Scientist	Bobbs
Stevenson	Kit Carson, Boy Trapper	Bobbs
Stockard	Experiments for Young Scientists	Little
Straus	Let's Experiment	Harper
Syme	Balboa, Finder of the Pacific	Morrow
Tousey	Davy Crockett	Whitman
Travers	Mary Poppins	Harcourt
U. S. Comm. for UNICEF	Hi Neighbor (Book 7)	Hastings
Vivian	Science Games for Children	Sterling
Walden	Nutcracker	Lippincott
Waller	Electricity: A Book To Begin On	Holt
Warner	Mike's Mystery	Whitman
Watson	Bear Country	Singer
Wattenberg	Story of Harbors	Sterling
Webber	Bits That Grow Big	Scott
Wellman	Earthquakes and Volcanoes	Day
Wheeler	Frederic Chopin, Son of Poland	Dutton

Author	Title	Publisher
White	Charlotte's Web	Harper
Widdemer	Washington Irving, Boy of Old New York	Bobbs
Wilkie	Daniel Boone Taming the Wilds	Garrard
Williams	Danny Dunn and the Heat Ray	McGraw
Williamson	First Book of Bugs	Watts
Wilson	Herbert	Knopf
Woods	Up-and-Down Inventor	Bobbs
Young	Secret of Stone House Farm	Harcourt
Zim	Universe	Morrow

JUNIOR HIGH SCHOOL

Author	Title	Publisher
Aardema	Tales From the Story Hat	Coward
Adler	Color in Your Life	Day
Adler	Weather in Your Life	Day
Alcott	Little Men	Macmillan
American Heritage Magazine	Great Days of the Circus	American Heritage
American Heritage Magazine	Men of Science and Invention	American Heritage
American Heritage Magazine	Story of Yankee Whaling	American Heritage
Anderson	First Under the North Pole	World
Applegate	First Book of Language	World
Arnold	Marvels of the Sea and Shore	Abelard
Arnott	African Myths and Legends	Walck
Arnov	Oceans of the World	Bobbs
Asimov	Words From the Myths	Houghton
Baker	Young Potter	Warne
Baldwin	America's Buried Past	Putnam

Author	Title	Publisher
Ball	Wood Carving for Fun and Profit	Exposition
Bank-Jensen	Play with Paper	Macmillan
Barr	Young Scientist Looks at Skyscrapers	McGraw
Baumann	Caves of the Great Hunters	Pantheon
Bedard	Gymnastics for Boys	Follett
Beeler	Experiments in Sound	Crowell
Bendick	Electronics for Young People	McGraw
Berger	Science and Music	McGraw
Bethers	Ports of Adventure	Hastings
Bevans	Book of Sea Shells	Doubleday
Bontemps	Story of the Negro	Knopf
Borer	Mankind in the Making	Warne
Bradley	Here's How It Works	Lippincott
Branley	Guide to Outer Space	Home
Brown	Rain Forest	Coward
Bryant	Party ABC's	Bobbs
Buehr	First Book of Machines	Watts
Buehr	Volcano!	Morrow
Bulfinch	Mythology	Crowell
Bunche	Instruments of the Orchestra	Golden
Burton	Life Story	Houghton
Cahn	Story of Writing	Harvey
Chester	Rockets and Spacecraft of the World	Norton
Clumer	Case of the Missing Link	Basic Books
Collins	Wonders of Geology	Putnam
Colum	Roofs of Gold	Macmillan
Cooke	Flights That Made History	Putnam
Cooke	How Books Are Made	Dodd
Cooper	Silkworms and Science	Harcourt
Courlander	Tiger's Whisker and Other Tales and Legends from Asia and the Pacific	Harcourt
Crocker	Party Book	Golden
Dareff	First Microscope	Parents
Darling	Before and After Dinosaurs	Morrow
D'Aulaire	Book of Greek Myths	Doubleday
David	Electricity in Your Life	Prentice
DeCamp	Energy and Power	Golden
DeCamp	Man and Power	Golden

Author	Title	Publisher
Deutsch	More Tales of Faraway Folk	Harper
Dietz	All About Great Medical Discoveries	Random
Dilger	Finding Out About Birds	Home
Dobler	Great Rulers of the African Past	Doubleday
Dodge	Plants That Changed the World	Little
Elting	Secret Story of Pueblo Bonito	Harvey
Epstein	First Book of the United Nations	Watts
Farb	Story of Life	Harvey
Fenton	In Prehistoric Seas	Doubleday
Fermi	Story of Atomic Energy	Random
Fichter	Reptiles and Their Way of Life	Golden
Fox	Birds Will Come to You	Reilly
Freeman	All About Sound and Ultrasonics	Random
Freund	Jewels for a Crown: The Story of the Chagall Windows	McGraw
Friedman	Man in the Making	Putnam
Frost	You Come Too	Holt
Gag	Wish for Mimi	Holt
Garstang	Basketball the Modern Way	Sterling
Giles	Toughen Up	Putnam
Glubok	Art of Ancient Greece	Atheneum
Goldston	Legend of the Cid	Bobbs
Goodwin	All About Rockets and Space	Random
Grant	Wonder World of Microbes	McGraw
Gregor	Short Story of the Universe	Macmillan
Hapgood	Great Mysteries of the Earth	Putnam
Hartwell	Something for Laurie	Holt
Hazeltine	Hero Tales From Many Lands	Abingdon
Herbert	Water: Beginning Science with Mr. Wizard	Doubleday
Hodges	Three Princes of Serendip	Atheneum
Hoffman	Book of Big Birds	Doubleday
Hogben	Wonderful World of Communication	Doubleday
Hoke	First Book of the Jungle	Watts
Holland	Casey Jones Rides Vanity	Little
Howard	Puppet and Pantomime	Sterling

Author	Title	Publisher
Hughes	Pictorial History of the Negro in America	Crown
Hyde	Animals in Science: Saving Lives Through Research	McGraw
Hyde	This Crowded Planet	McGraw
Irving	Electromagnetic Waves	Knopf
Ish-Kishor	Tales From Wise Men	Lippincott
Jackson	Sports Cars	Walck
Janson	Story of Painting for Young People	Abrams
Jeanes	Desert Beauty	Follett
Johnson	Supreme Court	Morrow
Joy	Race Between Food and People	Coward
Jupo	Sports, Sports Everywhere	Dodd
Kane	Tale of a Wood	Knopf
Kaplan	Posers	Harper
Kavaler	Artificial World Around Us	Day
Kavaler	Wonders of Algae	Day
Kay	Secrets of the Dolphin	Macmillan
Kieran	Introduction to Birds	Doubleday
Kipling	Jungle Book	Doubleday
Kjelgaard	Fawn in the Winter and Other Stories	Dodd
Kohn	Computers at Your Service	Prentice
Kohn	Peaceful Atom	Prentice
Lampman	Shy Stefosairis of Indian Springs	Doubleday
Lang	New Star in the Big Cage	Lippincott
Lavine	Wonders of the Anthill	Dodd
Leavitt	Fun Time Terrariums and Aquariums	Children's
Lewellen	Understanding Electronics, From Vacuum Tube to Thinking Machine	Crowell
Lewis	New World of Plastics	Dodd
Life Magazine	Prehistoric Animals	Golden
Lyons	Smoke Rings	Harcourt

Author	Title	Publisher
MacLeod	Cheryl Downing, School Nurse	Messner
MacPherson	Great Racing Drivers	Putnam
Malcomson	Farm Dog	Little
Maloney	Story of Cameras	Sterling
Mann	How Things Work	Crowell
Marcus	First Book of Glaciers	Watts
Mark	Physics Lab of Your Own	Houghton
Martin	Conquest of Disease	Coward
Matthews	Exploring the World of Fossils	Children's
Matzdorff	Limpy	Hale
McAllister	Easy Steps to Safe Swimming	Vantage
McAlpine	Japanese Tales and Legends	Walck
McElfresh	Summer Change	Bobbs
Meyer	Water at Work	World
Milgrom	Explorations in Science	Dutton
Mindlin	Strange Animals	Bobbs
Montgomery	McNulty's Holiday	Duell
Moore	First Book of Painting	Watts
Morgan	First Electrical Book for Boys	Scribner
Newcomb	Alchemy to Atoms	Putnam
Newell	Mary Ellis, Student Nurse	Harper
Ogg	26 Letters	Crowell
Pastore	Dynamite Under the Alps: The Challenge of the Mont Blanc Tunnel	Coward
Peterson	How to Know the Birds	Houghton
Powers	Cave Dwellers in the Old Stone Age	Coward
Rainwater	Vision	Golden
Riedman	World Provider: The Story of Grass	Abelard
Roland	Song of Roland	Random
Rosenfeld	Magic of Electricity: 100 Experiments with Batteries	Lothrop
Ruchlis	Wonder of Heat Energy	Harper
Sandburg	Wind Song	Harcourt
Sanderson	Continent We Live On	Random
Savory	Zulu Fireside Tales	Hastings

Author	Title	Publisher
Scheele	Earliest Americans	World
Selsam	Plants That Move	Morrow
Shapiro	Wide World Cookbook	Little
Shelton	Flights of the Astronauts	Little
Simon	Wonders of the Butterfly World	Dodd
Slobodkin	First Book of Drawing	Watts
Smith	Mathematics: The Language of Science	Putnam
Sootin	Light Experiments	Norton
Soule	Maybe Monsters	Putnam
Spencer	Made in Japan	Knopf
Sperry	Challenge of Aab	Harper
Stambler	Breath of Life: The Story of Our Atmosphere	Putnam
Sterling	Lift Every Voice	Doubleday
Suggs	Modern Discoveries in Archaeology	Crowell
Swift	Wonderful World of Plants and Flowers	Home
Temkin	Jinny Williams: Library Assistant	Messner
Unesco	700 Science Experiments for Everyone	Doubleday
Untermeyer	World's Great Stories	Lippincott
Vogel	Ocean Harvest: The Future of Oceanography	Knopf
Wadsworth	Paul Bunyan and His Great Blue Ox	Doubleday
Wakeman	Wonders of the World	Dodd
Waller	Electricity: A Book to Begin On	Holt
Watson	Giant Golden Book of Dinosaurs and Other Prehistoric Animals	Golden
Weart	Story of Your Brain and Nerves	Coward
Wolfe	Deepest Hole in the World	Putnam
Young	Ceramics: Here Is Your Hobby	Putnam
Young	Sewing Book	Lippincott

Author	Title	Publisher
Zaidenberg	How to Draw Historic and Modern Bridges	Abelard
Zim	Universe	Morrow

HIGH SCHOOL

Author	Title	Publisher
Adler, B.	Churchill Wit	Coward
Adler, I.	Elementary Mathematics of the Atom	Day
Allen, B.	Mind Your Manners	Lippincott
Allen, T.	Quest: Report on Extraterrestrial Life	Chilton
Alpert	Barrymores	Dial
Ambler	To Catch a Spy	Atheneum
American Assembly	Outer Space Prospects for Man and Society	Prentice
Asimov	Greeks	Houghton
Auchincloss	Indifferent Children	Prentice
Axelrod	Tropical Fish Book	Arco
Bailyn	Pamphlets of the American Revolution	Harvard University
Barnes	Man with the Red and Green Eyes	Dutton
Beatty	Facing the Big Cats	Doubleday
Beauchamp	Iroquois Folk Lore: Gathered From the Six Nations of New York	Friedman
Beiser	Story of the Earth's Magnetic Field	Dutton
Bernstein	Watch Your Language	Atheneum
Bova	Star Watchman	Holt
Bowman	Guide to Crete	Pantheon
Brooks	An Autobiography	Dutton
Brundage	Empire of the Inca	University of Oklahoma
Buckmaster	Freedom Bound	Macmillan
Burbank	Sherwood Anderson	Twayne
Butcher	Our National Parks in Color	Potter
Caldwell	Pillar of Iron	Doubleday
Carmichael	James Smithson and the Smithsonian Story	Putnam
Catton	Never Call Retreat	Doubleday
Chavarria	Traditional India	Prentice

Author	Title	Publisher
Christie	Surprise! Surprise!	Dodd
Churchill	Churchill's History of the English Speaking People	Dodd
Chute	One Touch of Nature and Other Stories	Dutton
Cichy	Great Ages of Architecture	Putnam
Clemens (C. Neider, ed.)	Complete Novels of Mark Twain	Doubleday
Cole	Islands in Space	Chilton
Commager	Living Ideas in America	Harper
Conant	Shaping Educational Policy	McGraw
Cook	Exploring Under the Sea	Abelard
Cormack	Imhotep	Watts
Crowther	Six Great Doctors	Hamish
Cruickshank	Thoreau on Birds	McGraw
Dane	Godson	Norton
Daniel	Idea of Prehistory	World
Daugherty	Walt Whitman's America	World
Day	History of English Literature: 1837 to the Present	Doubleday
Deighton	Funeral in Berlin	Putnam
D'Haucourt	Life in the Middle Ages	Walker
Diamond	World of Probability: Statistics in Science	Basic
Dickinson	Empire and Nation	Prentice
Divine	Six Great Explorers	Hamish
Dolan	Yankee Peddlers of Early America	Potter
Dreiser	Best Short Stories of Theodore Dreiser	World
Duggan	Count Bohemond	Pantheon
DuMaurier	Flight of the Falcon	Doubleday
Dunlop	Automation and Technological Change	Prentice
Durham	Negro Cowboys	Dodd
Eckert	Great Auk	Little
Eichelberger	UN: The First Twenty Years	Harper
Ernst	Favorite Sleuths	Doubleday

Author	Title	Publisher
Fiene	Complete Guide to Oil Painting	Watson
Fisher	Exploring the Heavens	Crowell
Forester	Gun	Dufour
Forsee	Pablo Casals: Cellist for Freedom	Crowell
Fribourg	Supreme Court in American History	Macrae
Friedson	Literature Through the Ages	Sterling
Garnett	Treasures of Yesterday	Doubleday
Gaskell	World Beneath the Oceans	Doubleday
Gies	Bridges and Men	Doubleday
Girl Scouts of America	Senior Girl Scouts Handbook	Girl Scouts of America
Gonzales	Tennis	Fleet
Griswold	Art of Burma	Crown
Gruen	Heart of Our Cities	Simon
Guicharnaud	Molière	Prentice
Halliday	Concise History of England	Viking
Halsey	Old New York Frontier	Friedman
Harper	I Came from the Stone Age	Dutton
Harte	Stories of the Early West	Platt
Harvey	Exploring Biology	Doubleday
Hatfield	Pleasures of Herbs	St. Martin's
Hentoff	Jazz Country	Harper
Hepburn	Complete Guide to New York City	Doubleday
Higbee	Farms and Farmers in an Urban Age	Twentieth Century
Highton	Home Book of Vegetarian Cookery	Roy
Hill	Birds of Cape Cod, Massachusetts	Morrow
Hodge	Adventurers	Doubleday
Horizon Magazine	Marco Polo's Adventures in China	Harper
Hoyt	Short Story of Science	Day
Human	Quotation Dictionary	Macmillan
Hutcheson	Literature of the Piano	Knopf
Huxtable	Classic New York	Doubleday
Hvass	Birds of the World	Dutton
Irving	History of New York	Twayne

Author	Title	Publisher
Jackson	Pictorial Guide to the Planets	Crowell
Jarrell	Lost World	Macmillan
Kelley	John Burroughs: Naturalist	Exposition
Kerans	World's Greatest Sea Adventures	Horizon
Kerner	Treasury of Lincoln Quotations	Doubleday
Kieran	Story of the Olympic Games	Lippincott
Kipling	Phantoms and Fantasies	Doubleday
Kittler	Hail To the Chief: Inauguration Days of Our Presidents	Chilton
Kraft	When Teenagers Take Care of Children	Macrae
Krutch	If You Don't Mind My Saying So	Sloane
Lal	Spiritual Stories from India	Tuttle
Lear	Kepler's Dream	University of California
Lesko	You and Your Boat	Lothrop
Lewis	Historical Long Island Paintings and Sketches	Long Island Forum
Lewis, A.	American Plays and Playwrights of the Contemporary Theatre	Crown
Lewis, N.	Modern Thesaurus of Synonyms	Doubleday
Lewis, N.	New Power with Words	Crowell
Life Nature Library	Animal Behavior	Time
Life Nature Library	Primates	Time
Life Science Library	Energy	Time
Life World Library	Mexico	Time
Life World Library	Tropical Africa	Time
Longsworth	Emily Dickinson	Crowell
Lorca	Five Plays: Comedies and Tragi-comedies	New Directions
Lothrop	Treasures of Ancient America	Skira
Lovell	Discovering the Universe	Harper
Ludovici	Origins of Language	Putnam

Author	Title	Publisher
Lundberg	Coming World Transformation	Doubleday
Lyman	Story of New York	Crown
Manley	Teen-Age Treasury of the Arts	Funk
Marsh	Best Sports Stories, 1965 Edition	Dutton
Martin	Nathaniel Hawthorne	Twayne
Masefield	Old Raiger and Other Verse	Macmillan
Masin	New Treasury of Sports Humor	Prentice
Matute	Lost Children (tr. from Spanish)	Macmillan
McGinley	Sixpence in Her Shoe	Macmillan
McKown	Mendeleyev and His Periodic Table	Messner
Medley	Chinese Art	Horizon
Mellersh	Boy's Book of the Wonders of Man	Roy
Meyersohn	Memorable Quotations of John F. Kennedy	Crowell
Michener	The Source	Random
Morin	Churchill: Portrait of Greatness	Prentice
Morris	Great Detective Stories	Hart
Morris	Great Humorous Stories	Hart
Morsberger	James Thurber	Twayne
Mosley	Haile Selassie: Conquering Lion	Prentice
Murray	Comedy Roundup for Teenage Actors	Plays
Musicano	Building and Operating Model Ships	Funk
Neal	From Spinning Wheel to Spacecraft	Messner
Neustadt	Presidential Power	Wiley
Newcomb	Miracle Plastics	Putnam
Niggli	Miracle for Mexico	New York Graphic
O'Faolain	I Remember! I Remember!	Little
Ornstein	ABC's of Languages and Linguistics	Chilton
Orr	Animal Kingdom	Macmillan
Palmer	My Game and Yours	Simon
Parr	Ferdinand Magellan, Circumnavigator	Crowell
Payne	Ancient Greece	Norton
Paz	Labyrinth of Solitude: Life and Thought in Mexico	Grove

Author	Title	Publisher
Pei	Story of Language	Lippincott
Perham	Ten Africans	Northwestern University
Poe	Poems of Edgar Allan Poe	Crowell
Poole	Scientists Who Work with Cameras	Dodd
Porter, C.	Our Indian Heritage: Profiles of Twelve Great Leaders	Chilton
Porter, K.	Ship of Fools	Little
Prevelakis	Sun of Death (tr. from Greek)	Simon
Prudden	Teenage Fitness	Harper
Rayback	Richards Atlas of New York State	Richards
Raymond	Good Housekeeping's Book of To-day's Etiquette	Harper
Rebikoff	Underwater Photography	Chilton
Remini	Election of Andrew Jackson	Lippincott
Richardson	Painting in America	Crowell
Robotti	Whaling and Old Salem	Fountainhead
Rockwell	Complete Guide to Successful Gardening	Doubleday
Ross	Weather	Lothrop
Ruskin	Spy for Liberty: Adventurous Life of Beaumarchais—Playwright and Secret Agent for the American Revolution	Pantheon
Ruth	Great Day in the West	University of Oklahoma
Scott	Scott's Last Expedition	Dodd
Seldin	Automation	Coward
Serullaz	French Impressionists: A Selection of Drawings	Shorewood
Shenton	History of the U. S. From 1865 to Present	Doubleday
Shenton	History of the U. S. to 1865	Doubleday
Siebert	Baseball	Sterling
Silverberg	Men Who Mastered the Atom	Putnam
Silverberg	Socrates	Putnam
Simon	Mathematical Magic	Scribner
Sitwell	Music and Ceremonies	Vanguard

Author	Title	Publisher
Small	Best of True West	Messner
Smith, B.	Men of Peace	Lippincott
Smith, H.	World's Great Bridges	Harper
Snow	Mysterious Tales of the New England Coast	Dodd
Sports Illustrated	Book of Safe Driving	Lippincott
Stefansson	Discovery: The Autobiography of Vilhjalmur Stefansson	McGraw
Stevenson	Great Tales of Mystery and Adventure	Platt
Strauss	New Ways to Better Meetings	Viking
Swift	Gulliver's Travels	Doubleday
Talese	New York: A Serendipiter's Journey	Harper
Tapply	Sportsman's Notebook	Holt
Taylor	Two Roads to Guadalupe	Doubleday
Teale	Audubon's Wildlife	Viking
Terrell	Furs by Astor	Morrow
Thomas	Computers	Holt
Tilden	Following the Frontier	Knopf
Tracy	200 Main Course Dishes	Scribner
Trevine	Juan de Pareja	Farrar
UNICEF	Children of Developing Countries	World
Vermes	Girl's Book of Personal Development	Associated Press
Verne	20,000 Leagues Under the Sea and Around the Moon	Platt
Walker	Mammals of the World	Johns Hopkins Press
Waugh	Family of Islands	Doubleday
Wharton	Edith Wharton Reader	Scribner
White	Making of the President	Atheneum
Wise	·Harriet Beecher Stowe	Putnam
Wood	Trust Thyself: Life of Ralph Waldo Emerson for the Young Reader	Pantheon
Young	Negro Firsts in Sports	Johnson

APPENDIX D
TEACHER-PREPARED MATERIALS

This appendix shows examples of useful materials prepared by teachers, based on the skill needs of pupils. Some of the topics used grew out of specific pupil interests. These teacher-prepared materials are adaptable to ditto sheets for each pupil, and to use on a chalkboard or transparency for the overhead projector. The materials can be easily adapted to older or younger students as required. They are made of the simplest materials: paper clips or paper fasteners, which serve to hold the cards in place; cardboard and colored papers; and staples to strengthen pockets and envelopes.

These materials have been used on different age and grade levels. Each chart shown is concerned with the study of a specific skill, though the teacher has in mind broader concomitant aims. For example, the specific goal for the students using the "How We Can Build Words" chart is to develop skill in attacking the meaning of new words. The teacher's aim is to develop the students' vocabulary through knowledge of the derivation of words by way of reference to dictionary, encyclopedia, and books on the (semantic) origin of words.

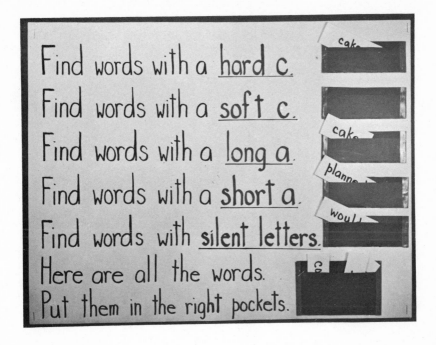

1. Phonics Skills

This chart was designed to reinforce phonics skills. The pupil selects a card from the lower right hand pocket and places it in the appropriate pocket.

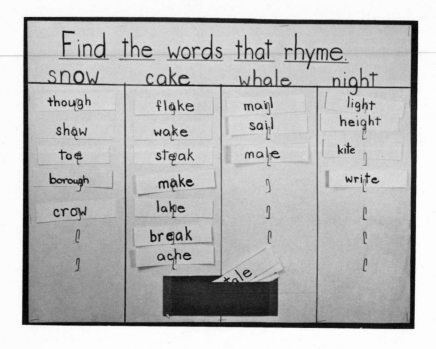

2. Find the Words that Rhyme

This chart was developed to strengthen auditory discrimination skills. The pupil takes a card from the pocket at the bottom of the chart and places it in the correct column.

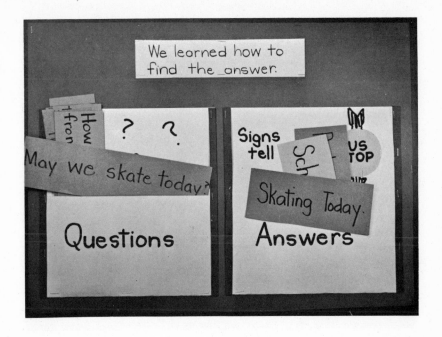

3. We Learned How to Find the Answer

This chart was designed to increase the pupil's comprehension skills. The student selects a card from the "question" pocket and then finds the answer in the cards from the "answer" pocket.

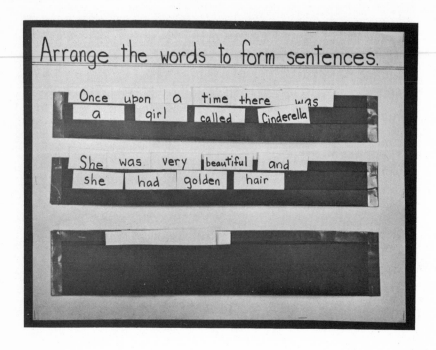

Arrange the words to form sentences.

Once upon a time there was
a girl called Cinderella

She was very beautiful and
she had golden hair

4. Arrange the Words to Form Sentences

This was developed to increase the pupil's comprehension skills. The student selects an envelope containing a series of word cards from the lower pocket. He then arranges these words in an upper pocket to form a sentence.

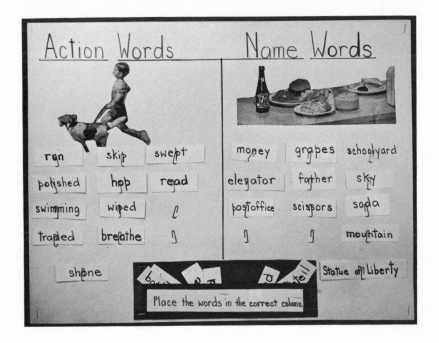

5. Action Words — Name Words

This chart was developed to further the pupil's knowledge of the distinctions in word usage. This is, also, an initial step in the introduction of grammar. The student selects a card from the pocket at the bottom of the chart and attaches it on the correct side.

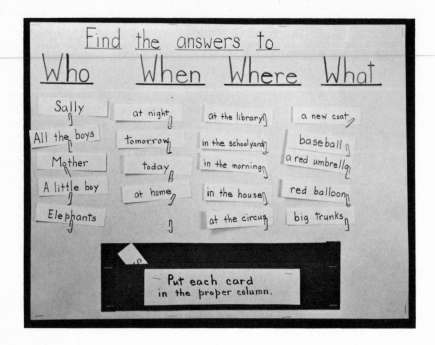

6. Find the Answers to Who? When? Where? What?

This chart was created to help pupils with comprehension skills. The student selects a card from the pocket at the bottom of the chart and places it in the appropriate column.

What? Where? Who? When? How?

Here are some parts of sentences. Each part answers one of the questions above. Next to each one, place the correct question card.

1. the two girls
2. next year
3. to the baseball game
4. on foot
5. at home
6. with all his might
7. during the storm
8. on the sidewalk

7. What? Where? Who? When? How?

This chart was designed to further pupils' comprehension skills. The student reads a part of a sentence which appears on the chart and then places in the pocket the card which is suitable—What, Where, Who, When, How.

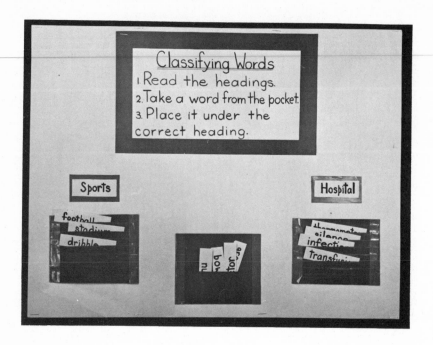

8. Classifying Words

This chart was created as a means to increase vocabulary. The pupil selects a card from the middle pocket and then places the card in the pocket under the correct category.

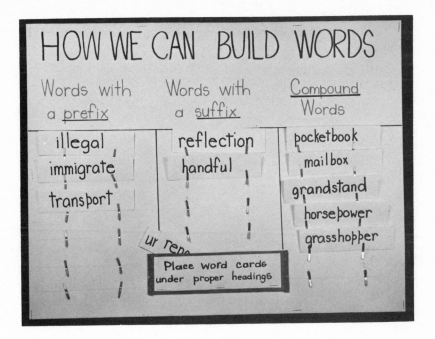

9. How We Can Build Words

This chart was developed to increase pupils' vocabulary and word-building knowledge. The student selects a card from the pocket at the bottom and places it in the appropriate column.

Newspapers are filled with news stories.
As you read them you will usually find answers
to four questions.

Who was concerned with the event?
What happened?
When did it happen?
Where did it happen?

Find the answers
to the 4 questions
in these news stories.

10. Newspapers Are Filled with News Stories

This chart was developed to improve pupils' comprehension skills. The student selects a newspaper clipping (which has been mounted) from the lower pocket. He reads to find the answers to the four questions that appear on the chart.

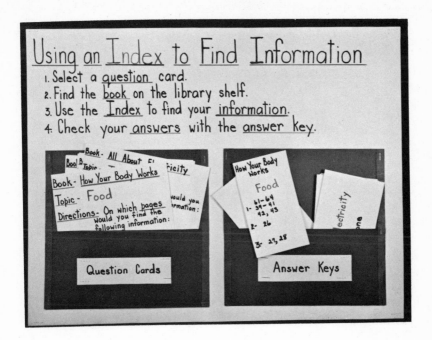

11. Using an Index to Find Information

This chart was designed to increase pupils' work-study skills. The student selects a question card from the pocket. On the library shelf he locates a book in which the answer can be found. By using the index the pupil then finds the pages which will answer the question. This chart is self-correcting. The pupil then takes the answer card out of the answer key pocket and checks himself.

The Use of Reference Materials

Reference or resource materials are among our most valuable sources of information. Among them are atlases, almanacs, histories, geographies, dictionaries, "Bartlett's Familiar Quotations", "Reader's Guide to Periodical Literature", "Who's Who", "Who's America".

Who said, "Give me liberty, or give me death"?

Bartlett's Quotations

Read the question

Here's the answer

12. The Use of Reference Material

This chart was created to introduce the pupil to research skills. The student selects a card from the "Read the Question" pocket. In the "Here's the Answer" pocket he finds the card containing the reference in which he would locate the answer.